THE ROMAN VILLA AT LLANTWIT MAJOR

The Roman Villa at Llantwit Major

Dr David T. Rogers
BSc BPharm(Hons) PhD MRSB

First published in 2020
© text: Dr David T. Rogers

All rights reserved. No part of this publication
may be reproduced, stored in a retrieval system,
or transmitted in any form or by any means, electronic,
electrostatic, magnetic tape, mechanical, photocopying,
recording, or otherwise, without prior permission
of the authors of the works herein.

ISBN: 978-1-84524-307-4

Cover design: Eleri Owen

Published by Gwasg Carreg Gwalch,
12 Iard yr Orsaf, Llanrwst, Wales LL26 0EH
tel: 01492 642031
email: books@carreg-gwalch.cymru
website: www.carreg-gwalch.cymru

To Michelle, Charlotte and Victoria.

'Nothing has such power to broaden the mind as the ability to investigate systematically.'
(Marcus Aurelius 121-180 CE)

About the author

David Rogers was born into a mining family in Gelligroes Village, Pontllanfraith, Monmouthshire. Both his paternal and maternal lineage consists of three generations of colliers preceded by a long lineage of agricultural and manual workers. Educated at Pontllanfraith Grammar Technical School he went on to study pharmacy at the Welsh School of Pharmacy, University of Wales Institute of Science and Technology, Cardiff. On completion of his Bachelor of Pharmacy honours degree he accepted a staff position at the Welsh School of Pharmacy engaging in antibiotic research for which he was awarded the degree of Doctor of Philosophy. He subsequently held various temporary lectureships and post-doctoral research positions, before moving into business as a community pharmacist. During the latter years of his business career he read a Bachelor of Science degree with the Open University and went on to teach with them as an Associate Lecturer. David is a member of the Royal Society of Biology and an amateur astronomer and microscopist. His range of interests are varied and include family history research, the history of science, model railway construction, gardening and painting in acrylic media. He and his wife Michelle live in Llantwit Major and have two daughters Charlotte and Victoria. It was a combination of interest in Roman and local history which provided the stimulus for his research into the Llantwit Major villa remains.

Content

Acknowledgements	8
Introduction	9
The Llantwit Major Villa	11
Chapter 1 Preliminary Excavation	15
Chapter 2 The 1888 Excavations	22
Chapter 3 The Villa Revealed	49
Chapter 4 The 1933 Attempt to Re-open the Villa Site	68
Chapter 5 The 1938–1948 Excavations	74
Chapter 6 The 1971 Excavations	122
Chapter 7 The 1981 Attempt to Re-open Caermead	127
Principal Characters Involved with the Villa Excavations	131
Notes	140
Further Reading	143
Acknowledgement for Figures	144

Acknowledgements

The Glamorgan Archives
Cardiff University Arts and Social Studies Library
Bridgend Local Studies Library
I am grateful to the following people for their help and assistance in making this book possible. Dr Peter and Dr Sue Dickson for reading the first draft, making constructive criticism and providing advice on amendments. Mrs Christine Young for reading a subsequent draft, suggested alterations and provision of background information on local characters involved with the excavations. Dr Tom Carnduff for reading the final proof. The Llantwit Major Local History Society Archive and its archivist Mr Nigel Williams for access to and provision of significant original documentation and photographs. The Archaeology Department of the National Museum of Wales, Cardiff for access to Dr Nash-Williams original field notebook and personal papers. Mr and Mrs Llewellyn of Morfa Farm, who generously allowed me to examine the original deeds of the property and granted access to Caermead on numerous occasions. Utrecht University Student Services and Faculty of Humanities, Holland for searching and providing information on Dr J.J.Fraenkel. Everyone at Gwasg Carreg Gwalch publishers for their assistance in bringing the manuscript to print. Finally, to my wife Michelle for her support and encouragement to undertake and bring the research to fruition in this book.

Introduction

Roman villas in Britain varied in complexity from palatial abodes such as Woodchester in Gloucester, with its grand mosaic floor and adornments, to more modest farmhouses with working outbuildings. This diversity could not only be a consequence of the wealth of the villa owner, but also due to evolution of the villa over the four hundred years of Roman rule. Many sites began as a modest Iron Age round house, and evolved into a cottage style oblong structure with a pitched roof under Roman influence. Even the simplest villa, with its separate rooms afforded a privacy that would have been previously unknown to the indigenous population. This simple structure would have formed the nucleus for a grander establishment which might evolve into a series of joined stone buildings, acquiring a colonnade and a courtyard as prosperity increased. Yet, although a degree of grandeur and comfort characterised the Roman villa, in essence they were foremost a working farm, producing a wide range of products and agricultural goods. In general terms, the location chosen for a villa embraced the two fundamental criteria of good communications and surrounding productive agricultural land. The rich farmland of the Vale of Glamorgan, lent itself readily to the establishment of a villa at Llantwit Major, and from here, the villa's agricultural output could be moved to the nearby Roman town of Cowbridge. The Roman road, the Via Julia, from Cardiff to Neath (Nidum) thought to have passed through Cowbridge, would have facilitated distribution of produce onwards to a much wider area. The movement of goods to and from the villa would also have benefited from its proximity to the Bristol Channel, where settlements along the South Wales snd West Country coast would be easily accessible by boat.

A cursory glance at a map of the locations of Roman villas in Britain would show an obvious concentration in England, particularly in the south eastern areas. Until recently, in South Wales only a few examples were known, principally Whitton, near Barry, Ely near Cardiff and the Llantwit Major villa. The antiquarians of the nineteenth century regarded Llantwit as the most westerly example of a Roman villa in the province, considering it to be located on the fringes of safe Roman influence. However, with the use of modern aerial survey equipment, a range of more westerly sites have been identified such as Dan-y-graig Porthcawl, Trelissey in Amroth, Pembrokeshire, and Abermagwr, Aberystwyth. In comparison to these examples, the villa at Llantwit although losing its title as the most westerly, still retains prominence for its size, quality of construction and degree of luxury.

The Llantwit Major Villa

To the north-north-west of the town of Llantwit Major in a field known as Caermead[1], lie the remains of a Roman villa of considerable size and archaeological importance. Today, although the villa remains buried, its presence can be identified on the landscape as a series of distinct undulations and irregularities (Figure 1). Until the last part of the eighteenth century however, local verbal testimony suggested that the walls of the villa remained some four to five feet above ground level in several places as the first excavator John Storrie, recorded in his excavation note book of 1888. '*William Powell, aged 91, now living in Llantwit, told me on the 13th October 1888, that when a lad of 12 years or so, he distinctly remembers the walls of the Roman buildings we have now discovered, still standing four or five feet high in several places, and another man told him he had seen a red pavement in sight about the same time.*' Unfortunately, over a twenty year period during the seventeen hundreds, a local limekiln owner, Humphrey Dembrey, was responsible for removing great quantities of the walling for burning. Because the stones did not require cleaning, and thus were suitable for immediate use in the kiln, they were attractive to Mr Dembury as a cost effective fuel. The result of Dembrey's actions was that the remains of a villa that had stood for over thirteen hundred years was dismantled and destroyed in a mere two decades, as recounted to Storrie by a local inhabitant.

It was also known that houses with carved stones had been found there, (Caermead) for I found a man still living, whose father had been in the employ of Humphrey Dembrey, who was a

Caermead today looking east. (Figure 1a)

Part of the villa walls exposed during the hot summer of 2018. (Figure 1b)

tenant of the then Lord Bute. This Humphrey Dembrey has a lime kiln near the spot where the house of Daniel Davis, J.P., has been built, and for a period of over twenty years he burnt limestone from the old walls, giving as his reason, that the stones there were all ready for burning, having no shale or "mother" attached, and so saving the labour of cleaning them, which had to be done when stones quarried from the natural bed had to be used. This man can distinctly recollect his father telling how Mr Dembrey preferred the carved stones for burning into lime, and that he had hauled great quantities of carved stones to the kiln. Dembrey died in 1795, see his gravestone near door of Llantwit Church.' (Storrie, J. 1888)

Humphrey Dembrey died on 20th of March 1795, aged sixty three years and is buried in the graveyard of St Illtuds Church in Llantwit Major just opposite the South Door (Figure 2). His dismantling of the villa's considerable remaining structure above ground level, in effect denied the area of a unique glimpse of Roman life in rural South Wales. Storrie himself was under no illusion as to the extent of the damage and loss of artefacts that Dembrey's dismantling had inflicted on the villa's remains. *'This I set down as quite incredible at the time but it is just possible from what we now know that this Dembrey may have burnt nearly the whole of the gravestones, alters etc belonging to the place'.* (Storrie, J. 1888)

In the opening pages of his notebook, Storrie mentions the location of Dembrey's limekiln as being near the house of Daniel Davis, and subsequently, he refers to this residence as Morfa House. On the 1891 census (RG12, Ed 4, Piece 4453, Folio 58, Page 4.) Daniel Davis is listed as a sixty one year old retired farmer/magistrate residing at Morfa with his wife, daughter and domestic servant. Morfa House is clearly marked on the Ordnance Survey maps of 1900, but labelled as Wetmoor Cottage on the earlier 1885 edition. Next to the cottage is a structure marked Limekiln. From Storrie's description and its proximity to the villa site, the limekiln adjacent to Morfa House is probably the kiln operated by Dembrey (Figure 3). The villa site, reduced to ground level after Dembrey's dismantling, remained largely undisturbed until it became the subject of an investigation by the academic community in the late nineteenth century, through the work of the aforementioned John Storrie. His excavation, followed by two more in the following century revealed evidence of a Romano-British villa of considerable size and luxury.

Gravestone of Humphrey Dembrey.
(Figure 2)

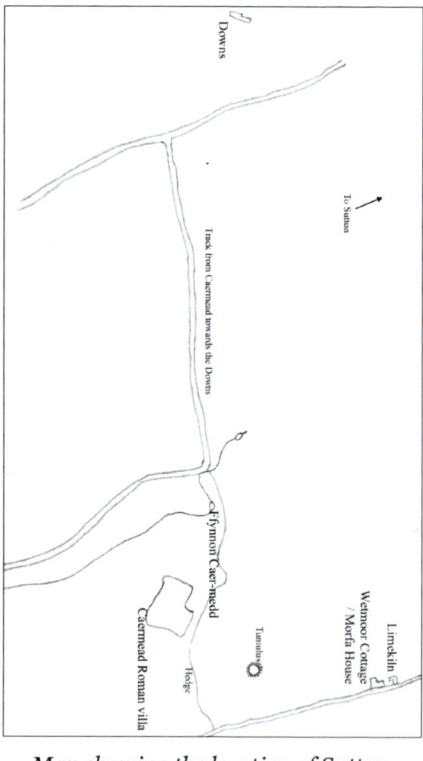

Map showing the location of Sutton,
The Downs, Caermead Field,
Morfa House and associated features.
(Figure 3)

Chapter 1

Preliminary Excavation

Mr John Storrie (Figure 4), the Curator of the Cardiff Museum, undertook the first archaeological excavations of the site in 1888, under the auspices of Cardiff's early scientific body, The Cardiff Naturalists' Society. Although Storrie did not conduct the first excavations at Caermead until August 1888, he had become aware of the villa site some eight years previously in July 1880, probably whilst on one of his holidays in Llantwit Major. During his stay he embarked on a visit to Sutton[1] to collect fossils from the Sutton Beds, when he met a Mr G.E. Robinson and spent some time in his company. *'Being a miserably wet day I stayed rather longer with him than I intended and night set in before I got half way to Llantwit, where my wife was then staying'*. On making his way back towards Llantwit Major, and becoming somewhat disorientated, Storrie began walking along the lane that led from the Downs[2] towards the Caermead area. During the course of his walk, the weather improved with the sky clearing, and the emerging moonlight illuminated the landscape, revealing the undulations on the terrain at the villa site. Being an experienced and observant naturalist, the field's unusual topography caught his attention and interest. *'The peculiar character of the field struck one very forcibly at the time'*. Continuing to Llantwit that evening he fully intended to retrace his path the following day to conduct a detailed examination of the field. However, he found difficulty in locating it during the daylight hours and it was some years later that he eventually re-discovered the site, as he explained in a lecture

to the Cardiff Naturalists' at Cardiff University in October 1888.
Mr Storrie determined to return next morning and explore, but the next morning he could not find the field of the curious mounds, nor could anyone in Llantwit-Major tell him anything of it or even its whereabouts. Three or four years later, however, Mr Storrie was botanising around Llantwit, and came upon the same field again, but having no tools with him, he was not able to do anything, and it was not until last year that he was able to carry out his wish of exploring the mounds, the curious character of which had so forcibly impressed his memory.
(*Western Mail 13th October 1888*)

Having located the site once again, Storrie approached the older inhabitants of the town in the hope of obtaining local knowledge as to the nature of the remains.

Mr Storrie's next step was to get hold of all the old men of the neighbourhood and endeavour to glean some information from them. In this he was fairly successful, for he learned that in the field walls had stood some hundred years ago, but the stones carted to a limekiln and burned into lime.
(*Western Mail 13th October 1888*).

Although, not all the information gleaned from members of the local community was as accurate as it first appeared as he later mentioned in his notebook. '*The mounds in the Garnmead (sic) were known to most of the old people in the neighbourhood as the "Old Barracks" which I at first took for a remarkable instance of tradition, handing down the military character of the buildings, but I soon found that the term "Old Barracks" is applied locally, not according to its usual sense, but to any article or house or even broken down animal*'. From this experience he appears to have learned a valuable lesson in the reliability of information imparted by the general populous. Professor Issac Newton's dictum to Dr Robert Hooke in 1689, is particularly applicable to the information provided to him on this occasion, *'Merely because someone says something could be so, it does not follow that it is so'*. A valuable piece of advice to every researcher, whatever the discipline.

Although Storrie had a natural interest in archaeology, his particular attention to Caermead may well have arisen, and been stimulated from a focus of archaeological research of the period, namely to determine the location of Bovium. This town mentioned

Photograph of John Storrie. T.L.Howe, Penarth, From the Public Library Journal, *(June 1901) Vol.3, Part 3, P.80.* (Figure 4)

in antiquarian documents was reputed to lie on the Roman road, the Via Julia, from Cardiff to Neath. His interest was motivated by a passage he refers to in his notebook simply as "Rees Vol. 18 p. 551" from which he quotes *'But the great object of antiquarian research in this part of the country is the station of Bovium'*. Finding its location would have been a significant achievement for Storrie, who had already examined a number of possible locations. *'For some years I have tried small explorations to endeavour to set at rest the long controversy as to the site of Bovium, and had made a trial at Llanmaes, Boverton, Liege Castle, near the Old Post and Mynydd-y-gaer, near Capel Llanbad-super-Montem but with very little success'*.

On the 17th of August 1887, whilst Storrie was staying in Llantwit for a fortnight holiday he returned to Caermead and performed a explorative dig on a cubic yard area of the site. The summer season of that year had been dry and Storrie had gained knowledge of a well in Caermead field which he noted yielded good quality, and quantities of water. He reasoned that any possible settlement, indicated by the mounds in the field, would need water, and siting it near such a spring would be logical. With this in mind he selected a point to dig midway between the well and the villa's location, in the hope that pots or utensils used for water carrying over an extended period, by past occupants would eventually suffer breakages. Thus, he would find their discarded remains along the water bearers route. The spring or well mentioned by Storrie was also referred to in a Western Mail article of 1888.

> *Excavations at Llantwit Major, The Palace of a Roman Praetor Exhumed, by Morien*[3]
> *To the west of the bath is the well which supplied the palace with water. It would appear as if the place were built on this spot on account of the splendid perennial spring of water, which in the Vale is peculiarly valuable. I am told that the old Roman arch over this well continued in good repair until last year. The water seems to be 3ft or 4ft deep, and it is said that last summer during the drought, this spring continued to give a full supply of the purest water.*
> (*Western Mail 12th September 1888*)

The Ordnance Survey maps of eighteen hundreds, show a number of springs and wells but they are all a considerable distance from the villa itself, making the moving of water difficult. On the Ordinance Survey map of 1885, in close proximity to the villa is what appears to be a water course and a spring labeled "Ffynnon Caer-medd". The Welsh word Ffynnon is translated as well, spring or fountain, and thus the full translation would be Fountain Fort Mead (Figure 3). The spring is conveniently sited to supply the villa's needs, particularly the bath house from its close proximity on the villa's western side. Morien's reference to a Roman Arch over the well in the newspaper article must be considered with caution as he cites no evidence to confirm this and although this structure may have originated from the Roman period, it could equally have been a medieval or much later construction.

Storrie's choice of area for a preliminary dig was fortuitous in that he unearthed twenty three pottery fragments; large quantities of limpet and periwinkle shells, fragments of human bone and charcoal, all of which indicated prior human occupation. Although the pottery was of four different kinds, some was unmistakably Roman, whilst other material was of a crude form produced without the aid of a potters wheel. He then proceeded to search the site for buried walls and utilising a steel rod, shaped like a walking stick, he eventually determined the rough position of each subterranean wall structure in the field. This initial dig, although showing archaeological promise of further revelations, had another unexpected and dramatic consequence, as the Western Mail reported.

> *Mr Storrie related an amusing incident which occurred to him at this period of his discovery, and the details of which he had learned a week or so after beginning this year. Whilst he was digging some person had watched him, and had informed the local constable that some man had dug a hole in the field and had buried what the imaginative informer believed the body of a baby. The constable re-opened the hole Mr Storrie had made and though he found nothing, for days after where ever Mr Storrie went, he was watched by the stern eye of the suspicious police-officer.*
> (*Western Mail* 13th October, 1888.)

In September 1887, Storrie reported the results of his preliminary finding to Dr C.T.Vachell, (Figure 5) of the Cardiff Naturalists' Society showing him the pottery and bone finds. Vachell brought Storrie's findings to the attention of the Cardiff Naturalists' Society Committee in their meeting of the 10th of February 1888, stating that opening of the Caermead site would probably yield good results. He proposed to the committee that he would communicate with the proprietor, a Mrs Murley of Bath, to seek permission for the Society to visit with a view to conducting excavations. Permission from the owners was subsequently confirmed by Vachell at the Naturalists' March meeting, and members of the Committee made a preliminary visit to the site from Cardiff by carriage, provided by Hunley and Son at a cost of £1-10. During their visit, an exploratory hole was dug which yielded encouraging results and prompted them at their July meeting to authorise an expenditure of £10 to fund the excavations. In addition, a Caer Worgan (sic) Sub-Committee was formed consisting of T.H.Thomas, Storrie, Proger, Nicholl of the Ham, C.Waldon, J.G.Corbett, Dr Vachell and the Hon. Sec., to oversee the excavations. This preliminary survey of the site was subsequently reported sometime later in the South Wales Echo newspaper.

> *Meeting of The Cardiff Library Committee*
> *Dr Vatchell said the whole neighbourhood of Llantwit was known to be filled with remains of great interest, and it was reported to some of them (the Naturalists' Society) that there was a curious large mound there which might be worth exploring. Fortunately they discovered that the field belonged to a relative of his, and she very kindly gave permission to make whatever excavations might be necessary. On first starting a number of gentlemen went down and saw the field, and it was decided to cut a trench through the centre of it. The trench was only about five feet wide, but already*

they had unearthed remains of great interest and importance. Mr Storrie assisted in the work during his holidays, and Mr Proger, junr., had also lent great assistance. He should like to see if the committee could not lend some aid. Everything found there would be placed in the Cardiff Museum.

Mr T.H.Thomas produced some sketches taken by him on the spot, and briefly described the nature of the discoveries made. In regard to what the place is, that, he said, was a matter of very great interest. About half-way between Cardiff and Neath there was once a Roman station, the site of which had been lost. However, here at this point they had found Roman remains which covered a very large space of ground, and they must be – he thought he might almost say positively – remains of a station. If so, it could hardly be other than the station he had referred to. It was said that the earliest church in Wales was inaugurated by the Emperor Theodosius[4], and this spot was understood to be the place where Theodosius's college stood. It was possible they might yet strike upon something which would tend to elucidate some of the problems surrounding the introduction of Christianity into the country.

... Some discussion followed on a suggestion thrown out that the committee should grant a small sum to assist in carrying on the work, and ultimately it was agreed to contribute £10 with that object.
(South Wales Echo 29th August 1888)

Dr Vachell. From The Cardiff Naturalists' Society Reports and Transactions, (1914) Vol. 47, pp. 1-6. (Figure 5)

Chapter 2

The 1888 Excavations

With the £10 grant Storrie was appointed Director of the Excavation and Mr T.W. Proger, the Naturalists' Societies Honorary Curator of Cardiff Museum (1833 to 1819), and engineer from Barry Docks, volunteered to provide assistance with the practical aspects. Armed with various excavation equipment and an old bell tent, hired for £3 from J.Smart and Co, the endeavour was ready to be commenced (Figure 6). During the course of the excavation it appeared that Storrie was not particularly enamoured with the bell tent as he noted. *'Old military tent made and stamped 1860. Rather old for service and most uncomfortable, most of the fastenings being of the most temporary character and many missing. I found a tent was but slightly better than the open air, as it was impossible to lock it up, and its contents and specimens were at the mercy of any impatient or persistent visitor whose fingers could not restrain from damage unless a constant guard was kept. No more tents for me if I should ever excavate any again'.*

The excavations began on Saturday 11th of August 1888 under the direction of Proger who secured the services of two men and a boy, to begin work whilst Storrie accompanied Dr Vachell on a Geologists Association of London field trip to Llandaff, Radyr Quarry and Pentych Iron Mine. Storrie arrived on site at the beginning of his summer holiday on the Monday morning at around 10 a.m., preceded by James Bell, Chief engineer for the Barry Dock and Railway Company, who had arrived some minutes before. Proger had made a start with a

The bell tent with Storrie and co-workers. From Storrie's original notebook. The young boy mentioned in the text is standing on the right hand side. (Figure 6)

small excavation, and Bell began a complete survey of the site which took most of the day. Bell took great pains to plot the terrain and ran a level from the Downs, half a mile distant, to derive an accurate plan and section which Storrie found to be invaluable during the course of his excavations. In the evening of that day, Storrie and Bell continued excavating the hole begun by Proger earlier, but they only unearthed charcoal, slates and burnt stones, indicating a fire at some point in the past, but no artefact of interest. Storrie, not feeling satisfied that the rudimentary excavation area begun by Proger had been judiciously chosen, made a fresh start on the following morning of Tuesday 14th of August. He choose, and pegged a starting point that would ensure an east-west diagonal section which intersected with the position of the greatest number of buried walls he had located on his previous visit in 1887. By doing this he hoped that his trenching would reveal the maximum amount of information possible about the buried structure.

To ensure that he was well outside the building line of the buried structures, he began trenching some 16 feet to the east of his first peg, which he had sited at the Morfa Lane end of the remains. By clearing the ground of turf and excavating to a depth of between 15 to 18 inches he found an undisturbed layer of rich black mould lying immediately on the dunstones, the local term for the highest arenaceous limestone of the Lias[1]. Excavations continued for some 10 feet before a small fragment of black pottery, similar to Upchuch[2] ware was found, and at the 19 feet point, a dry stone wall was unearthed behind which was a shallow ditch. For the rest of that day, nothing of consequence was revealed. However, early on the following morning, Wednesday 15th of August Storrie unearthed two fragments of Roman tile and what he described as several "peculiar" stones being "Jaspery" like in character. These were set aside for further examination, before he continued trenching through a dry stone wall structure.

On the morning of Tuesday the 16th he found more fragments of the black pottery, and on retracing his steps over the excavated trench he found his first coin, a third brass of Victorinus (268-270 CE) which he noted was not in very good condition. After breakfast of that day, Mr Bell arrived and spent the remainder of the morning revising and correcting the plan he had made of the site. At around twelve o'clock, whilst the helpers were at lunch, Bell and Storrie recommenced the excavations and unearthed an urn of crude pottery (Figure 7), crazed and considerably cracked, but still maintaining its shape. As an arrival of a deputation of the Cambrian Archaeological Association was expected, Storrie, carefully removed the urn and secured it safely on a wooden board. Further examination of the area revealed that when digging out foundations for the villa, Roman workmen had jarred the pot which was in a small tumulus, causing it to crack before it was covered by their continued digging. The Romans had been oblivious to its presence, possibly because the tumulus had been levelled

Photograph of trench with urn. From Storrie's original notebook.
(Figure 7a)

Drawing of the urn. From Storrie's original notebook. (Figure 7b)

sometime previously. On the arrival of the Cambrian Archaeologists the urn was opened to reveal only another small vessel and a small quantity of charcoal inside. Considerable discussion ensured as to its function as a possible cooking utensil or sepulchral, with Storrie advocating the latter as the most likely use. An unforeseen aspect of the find involved the field's tenant, Mr Evans who had a quite different view on the role of the urn.

This discovery created some fun, and also some trouble. It struck Mr Evans, the tenant that he had some claim upon this urn, which he believed contained gold. The breaking of the urn did not convince him that there was no hidden fortune, and to this day Mr Storrie thinks he believes the able excavator conjured the gold away. One visitor to the remains had propounded the theory that the urn was an old Roman cooking vessel, and was very indignant that no one credited his theory.'
(*Western Mail* 13th October, 1888)

Shortly after the Archaeologist's departure, Storrie discovered a small round brass boss approximately three quarters of an inch in diameter, but further trenching proved fruitless for the rest of the day. Working with Dr Vachell on the Friday, the digging was more rewarding as they found additional pieces of bronze, part of an armlet and a bronze fibula. On Saturday 18th the first room of the villa (Room 1), was encountered, located to the north of the excavation trench, and measuring 10 feet 4 inches wide and 16 feet 6 inches in length. Storrie described the walls of the room as fairly well built approximately 21 inches thick on the north and west sides. To the south was a wall, 27 inches thick, dividing it from a further room (Room 2) (Figure 8).

Excavations in Room 1 unearthed a peculiar roof pinnacle (Figure 9), carved from Bath Oolite stone, which had broken into four pieces; its lower part fashioned like a gutter, cut to fit the ridge of the roof, where Storrie thought it would act as a finial. In addition, lying the whole length of the room was a stone coping, channeled on its underside in a similar fashion to the pinnacle, which Storrie thought would have fitted the crest of the roof. Fragments of wall plaster remained from the wall finishes, painted Pompeiian Red and ornamented with lines of white. Large quantities of tiles were also present, and an old quern solidly built into one of the rooms door-quoins

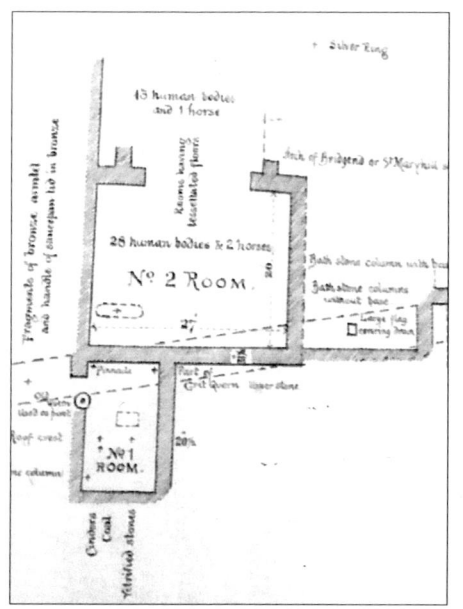

Plan of Rooms 1 and 2. After Storrie, J. (1888) The Cardiff Naturalists' Society Reports and Transactions, Vol.XX, Part II, p. 49. (Figure 8)

Roof pinnacle, drawing by T.H.Thomas. After Storrie, J. (1888) Cardiff Naturalists' Society Report and Transactions, Vol. XX, Part II, p. 49. (Figure 9)

The mosaic pavement. From Storrie's original notebook. (Figure 10)

which Storrie presumed had usage as a door pivot. Diagonally opposite this door was a masonry pillar, which Storrie surmised might have been a foundation for an anvil, since surrounding it were pieces of coal, charcoal, rough pieces of iron and vitrified stones. He concluded that the room had been used by artificers at some time. '*The room had the general appearance of a smithy, large quantities of iron cinder, one of the pieces with unmistakable coal buried in the body of the cinder showing that here, as at Caerwent, pit coal as well as charcoal had been used in working iron*' The only finished items found in the smithy detritus was a large iron staple around 6 inches in length and what appeared to be a spring-bolt for a door some 7.5 inches long. Clearance in the room also revealed the presence of many swine teeth and bones.

On Monday 20th work on the section trench was recommenced, revealing a room to the south of the line (Room 2) with a tessellated floor, although only a small portion of this remained intact (Figure 10). Hints of the floor's presence, in the form of odd tesserae, had been turning up during the previous days trenching. Now Storrie had first sight of the tesserae in situ, as a mosaic floor, together with a human skeleton on its surface.'*We had scarcely got a yard into it when we struck human bones, which proved to be those of a young man lying on his side partly crouched up, and with part of his head knocked in. I particularly noticed that the blow was lateral, and could not have been caused directly by pressure from above*'. In total, the skeletons of twenty five males, one female and two children of unknown sex were contained in this room. One skeleton was buried in what Storrie describes as the usual way, which presumably would be an east-west orientation. In the outer compartment of the room thirteen male skeletons were present, three rudely interned. The quoin near the entrance to Room 2 and a line of arch stones, dividing the room into two areas, were of St. Mary Hill sandstone, a fine textured sandstone that comes from St Mary Hill, in the Vale of Glamorgan. In the southern half of Room 2, considerably more of the tessellated pavement remained intact.

The Tessellated Pavement

This was an intricate pattern of brown, red, blue, white, light-green and dark sage tesserae, enclosed in a border of thirty one rows of brown sandstone tesserae on the northern edge and thirty five on the eastern and western sides. The tesserae were worked very close together and showed marks of having been washed in a reddish pigment, some of which still adhered to the tesserae themselves. To the inside of the brown border was a double fret-pattern strip of red, white and blue being 11.5 inches in width. Storrie surmised that it it dated from the time of Agricola, (circa 80 CE) but subsequent excavations indicated this dating to be inaccurate. The mosaic pavement itself had suffered considerable damage, especially to its centre regions, with around two thirds of it broken up completely. Storrie found several deep depressions present consistent with horse hoofs, and having uncovered three horse skeletons in the room, he conjectured that these were the cause of the scattering of the tesserae from the damaged area. *'And from the fact that three skeletons of horses have been found in this room it is inferred that the damage part has been kicked up by these horses, especially as most of the tesserae have been found on the spot, and not been removed as they would have been had they been intentionally broken up'*. From microscope examination, he proposed that the larger border tesserae were of Pennant sandstone, possibly of local origin, as many sources existed within a dozen or so miles of the villa. The blue tesserae he identified as mountain-limestone, being more crystalline in character than that of the local stone, whilst the red tesserae were of a brick like material and probably local in origin. The white tesserae were crystalline limestone and the green ones he thought may have been volcanic. The mosaic was a spectacular find and lent gravitas to the villa as a substantial and important abode.

The mosaic was unknown in Britain before the arrival of the Romans, and required a skilled tradesman to construct, generally by application of two common methods. One involved working in sections by laying *tesserae* on an area of wet mortar base, usually at the centre of the design and working outwards in subsequent sections using templates and set squared to ensure a quality finish. The second was a prefabrication technique where the *tesserae* were glued to a linen sheet with a water soluble adhesive in the desired pattern. A grouting of fine mortar was applied to the gaps between the tesserae and the whole panel protected by sandwiching between boards. Once the mortar floor had been laid it was scored to indicate the position of the mosaic. This allowed the panel to be positioned accurately, cloth upwards, onto the damp mortar before the lower board was carefully slid away. Once the floor had set, the linen was removed by dissolving the adhesive, to reveal the mosaic. An advantage of this method was that the pattern could be sketched on the linen before attaching the tesserae and hence standard designs could be shown to clients by the mosaic makers workshops.

A colour drawing of the mosaic was made at the site by Mr John John of Ashgrove, Llantwit Major (Figure 11), who subsequently marketed large (37 by 27 inch) lithographic copies, printed by Lavers Lithography, 51 Broad Street Bristol. The lithograph is a testament to his skills as a draughtsman and indeed presents a lovely renditioning of the mosaic, projecting a vision of its splendid, in-situ appearance. Mr John, also produced a four page pamphlet (Figure 12) to augment the lithographic copy which in addition to describing the discoveries made, cited endowments of its accuracy and artistic beauty by prominent figures, including John Storrie and members of the aristocracy.

On Tuesday 21st the excavation of the section trench was continued, albeit with some dissent from Proger. *'Kept straight on with the section (much against Mr Proger's will who wished to follow up the tesserae)'*. As the trench progressed, parts of a Bath Stone pillar were uncovered together with lots of tiles and sandstone slates, some with nails still present. On the Wednesday morning, the excavations took a diversion by moving from the main site to the adjoining field to the north. Having been granted permission by Daniel Davies, a start was made in the field adjoining Morfa House to drive a trench through the tumulus that existed there. Bell had made an elaborate survey of this previously, and together with Storrie had hopes of unearthing significant finds. The indigenous animal residents took a keen interest in the proceedings as Storrie's notes describe. *'We were much struck with the friendly character of the inhabitants, cattle, colts and sheep vied with each other in their curiosity as to what we were about and kept so close around us that we had barely elbow room to work'*. This enterprise proved fruitless, despite digging in a number of directions outwards from the tumulus. The only find was a few stones which Storrie described as curious in their structure, being extremely light, like cork. Finding no trace of human occupation they decided that it was a perfectly natural hillock and having filled it in, they returned to their original excavation. Why Storrie deviated from the main dig that was revealing so much of interest has a possible explanation in his notes and a newspaper article of the time. His notebook has an enlightening comment, written under a photograph of the partly revealed mosaic floor. *'First sight of the pattern of tessellated floor. When we had arrived at this stage we had orders to stop. I photographed it before covering it up'*. This was Monday 20th of August and in the

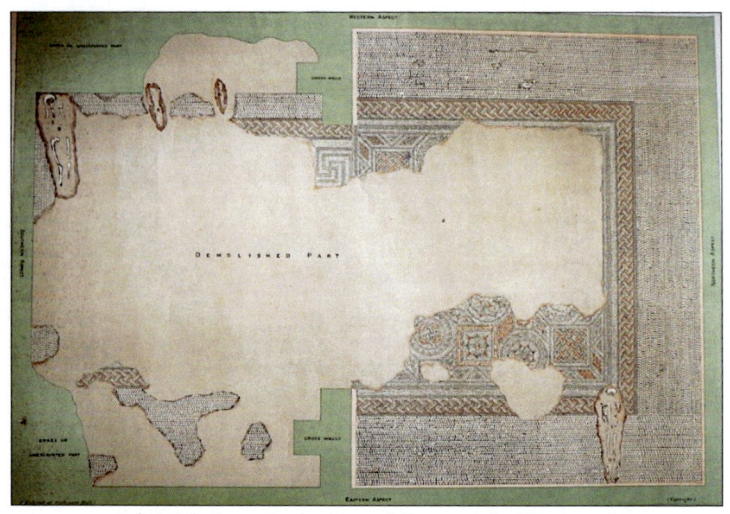

John John's reproduction of the mosaic. (Figure 11)

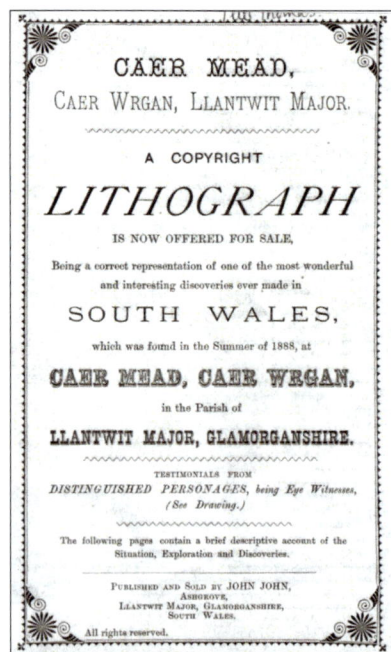

South Wales Daily News of 4th of September the following article appeared.

The Excavations at Llantwit
A Suspension and Renewal of Operations
Five More Skeletons Discovered
It will be remembered that on Wednesday last an article was published in the South Wales Daily News descriptive of the discovery of Roman remains near Llantwit Major. The search of the Cardiff

John John's Testimonial Pamphlet. (Figure 12)

Naturalists' Society, who had permission to make the excavations, was continued up till Saturday last, when their engaging efforts received a check from the ground landlady Mrs Murley of Bath. Mrs Murley requested a suspension of the work pending a consultation with her solicitor, and consequently Mr Storrie, curator of the Cardiff Museum, and Mr W.Proger, who were directing the investigation, had to close operations. It is satisfactory to be able to report now, however that the temporary prohibition has now been withdrawn at the instigation of Dr Vachell, and that the work is again in full progress.

The newspaper article indicates that work was recommenced after Dr Vachell's intervention, and the Naturalists' Society minutes from their September meeting provides further detail.

A meeting of the Caer Worgan (sic) Exploration Sub-committee was held this day at the Town Hall at 8pm,. Present, Dr Vachell, in the chair, Messers J.A.Corbett, J Storrie and the Hon.Sec.

Dr Vachell described what had been done up to the present time. The field belonged to Mrs Murley, and was let in the first instance to Mr Evans, who had sub let it, and letters from Mrs Murley and Mr Evans were read consenting to the working of the field for the purposes of exploration. Owing to the bad weather operations were not commenced until Aug 13th, and they were continued until Aug 31st when a letter was received from Mrs Murley asking that work should be stopped (sic) suspended until she had consulted her solicitor. A second letter was received on Sept ?[date crossed out] giving permission to continue digging until the 14th of September, the date of the inspection by the Cardiff Naturalist's Society, on which date work was stopped and since which nothing more had been done. (Cardiff Naturalists' Society Meeting Minutes 27th September 1888)

The Mrs Murley referred to in the newspaper article and Storrie's notes was the cousin of Dr Vachell. Although Vachell had approached his cousin in the first instance to obtain permission to excavate Caermead, it is clear from the Naturalists' Society minutes, that he does not appear to have contacted her personally in a formal manner to resolve the cessation of work.

> *On Sept 24th Mr J.A.Corbett, acting on behalf of Dr Vachell, wrote to Mr Matthews, Mrs Murley's solicitor, asking for a lease of the ground, to which letter no reply had been received up to this date.*
>
> (*Cardiff Naturalists' Society Minutes of the Meeting of 27th September 1888*)

At this juncture, the Naturalists' Society were confronted by the problem of how to complete the excavations, and recover the villa structures that the clearance had exposed before the onset of winter. To effect this they would need further permission to access the site. Fortunately, the legal position of the site was to their advantage, in that although Mrs Murley was the owner, she had let it to a Mr Evans who had subsequently sub-let it to a Mr Rees. This situation would allow the Naturalists to circumvent her cessation letter, by approaching the sublessee, which is what they appear to have done as detailed in their minutes.

> *To carry on the work, and to obtain power to make a charge for admittance to the field, Mr Storrie had taken a lease of the field for grass from Mr Rees, on behalf of the C.N.S up to February 2nd 1889, for the sum of £13.*
>
> (*Cardiff Naturalists' Society Minutes of the Meeting of 27th September 1888*)

Storrie's securing of a lease enabled himself and his colleagues to continue their presence on the field. In addition to this incident the Naturalists' also faced another problem. Although Storrie had devoted his summer holidays to the excavations he was still in salaried employment at the Museum, under the auspices of the Cardiff Free Library Committee and duty bound to return. In an effort to provide continuity with the overseeing of the site, Mr R.W.Atkinson the Honorary Secretary of the Cardiff Naturalists' Society wrote to the Cardiff Free Library Committee stressing the importance of the finds made and the continuing presence of Storrie on-site as a capable and responsible director of excavations. The Cardiff Naturalists' Society minutes of 27th of August recorded the details.

> *Dr. Vachell gave an account of the opening of the excavations at Caer Worgan, (sic) and a preliminary report from Mr Storrie was read explaining what had been done to that time. It was mentioned that Mr Storrie's holidays were almost at an end, and in view of the need of having some one to superintend the workmen it was resolved on the motion of Mr Ronnfeldt, seconded by Mr Seward, that the Free Library and Museum Committee be asked to give Mr Storrie leave of absence from the museum for two weeks to superintend the important excavations being carried out at Caer Worgan (sic). This was carried unanimously.*
>
> *It was further resolved on the motion of Mr Pettigrew seconded by Mr Ronnfeldt to increase the amount advanced by the Society by £5 to be repaid, if possible from the subscriptions to the Caer Worgan (sic) fund.*

The South Wales Echo reported on the progress made, and the Naturalists' approach to the Free Library Committee.

> *Meeting of The Cardiff Library Committee*
> *At a meeting of the free library, on Tuesday evening, the following letter from the secretary to the Naturalists' Society was read:-*

> *Dear Sir,—At a meeting of the committee of this society, held on Monday, the 27th inst. the following resolution was unanimously carried: "That the free library and museum committee be respectfully asked to grant leave of absence for a fortnight from the museum to Mr J.Storrie, the curator, for the purpose of superintending the important excavations now being carried on at Llantwit Major." The circumstances are briefly as follow: Near Llantwit Major is a field (Cae Morgan), (sic) in which a discovery of Roman remains has been made quite recently by this society, these remains consisting of stonework enclosing chambers used for various purposes, the coloured cement still remaining upon the walls of one of them; in another is a tessellated pavement, resembling that found at Caerwent, and a third chamber seems to have been without doubt a hypocaust, that is a heating chamber, used for the bath. Other very important finds have been made which lead the committee to believe that one of the most important discoveries in South Wales is now being made. To carry out the work thus far the committee of the C.N.S have made a grant of money, and as it is of the utmost importance that the work should be superintended by a responsible and capable person, they hope that the request conveyed in the resolution will be acceded to, seeing that all the objects found will enrich the Cardiff Museum.—I am, dear sir yours truly,*
> *R.W.Atkinson, Hon Sec. C.N.S.*
> *(South Wales Echo 29th August 1888)*

The letter had the desired effect, and in consideration of the work performed, and Storrie's handling of the excavations, the Cardiff Free Library Committee agreed to grant him a leave of absence to continue the supervision.

> *Mr Peter Price thought the explorations of so much importance as to warrant them in granting the services of Mr Storrie. He proposed that the application be acceded to.*

Mr Proger seconded the resolution, which was agreed to.
(Western Mail 29th August 1888)

Another problem that the Naturalists' faced was the considerable public attention that the excavations had produced. The local newspapers had reported widely on the progress of the work and their revealing finds. The consequence of the resulting public interest was that Storrie had to apportion around two hours during the day to allow visitors to gain access to the field, and receive explanations with regard to the villa's extent and the discoveries unearthed. However, not all the attention was of a civilised and passive nature, as the dig experienced an alleged disturbing incident where a group of men from the town were accused of gross vandalism of the exposed relics. Comprising some forty to fifty apparently drunken individuals, they gained access to the field and were soon allegedly displaying a total disregard for the exposed structures and causing damage to some. Storrie, in an effort to prevent further destruction, confronted the ringleaders but was physically assaulted and purportedly threatened with a knife. One of the group reportedly tore up tesserae from the tessellated pavement causing about a square foot of damage before being ordered off by Storrie. The whole affray had been precipitated by a local publican who ran a horse and trap to the site in order to acquire financial gain. Storrie's account described that he eventually restored a semblance of peace and afterwards involved the local constable, but the perpetrators were never prosecuted for their actions. The Western Mail newspaper published a letter from Storrie describing the event in detail.

The Interesting Discoveries at Llantwit Major
Outrageous Conduct Of Visitors

Vandalism Rampant
The Cardiff Curator Grossly Maltreated
Wanton Destruction of Roman Remains

As our readers are aware, interesting discoveries of Roman remains are being made at Llantwit Major, under the able superintendence of Mr John Storrie, the curator of Cardiff Museum. The accounts that have appeared in the Western Mail from time to time giving details of Mr Storrie's discoveries have awakened the interest of readers in all parts of the country. The article by "Morien" which appeared in our Wednesday issue, with illustrations of the tessellated pavement and Roman remains unearthed, tended to increase the interest that had been aroused. We are sorry therefore to have received the following letter from Mr Storrie, giving particulars of acts of vandalism and brutality which are a disgrace to the perpetrators:-

To The Editor of the Western Mail
SIR,- Would you allow me space in your valuable paper to protest against a state of things here which I think could not be reviled in the wilds of Ashantee! I have for some weeks been conducting an exploration of the Roman remains in a field about a mile north of Llantwit Major, and have devoted the whole of my summer holiday, and also incurred the cost of renting the field, solely for the purpose of elucidating the history of this place during the Roman and Romano-British period. The proprietor of the field granted me permission to dig, and the Cardiff Naturalists' Society supplied me with money to pay the workmen, and discoveries of great interest to Glamorganshire have been made. Although I had set apart two hours a day when visitors could come in and see the progress of the work gratuitously, on condition that no one should meddle with or destroy anything yet, after all this, a scene occurred here last

night which certainly was a disgrace to all concerned, and if repeated again will lead to the outside world to believe that Glamorgan is still uncivilised as the wilds of Central Africa. Shortly after five o'clock, the hour when visitors are admitted the whole place was invaded by a gang of about 40 or 50 rowdies, half drunk and foolhardy, who insisted upon walking over and jumping on the crumbling walls and pavement. I had met them on entering and explained fully how frail and tottering everything was. One would have thought that every aid and assistance would have been rendered me to preserve the walls and floor intact until steps could have been taken for their preservation, but the ways of the half-drunken men, when goaded on by a publican whose highest ambition is to run the ruins as a side show to a public-house and enable him to sell an extra cask or two of beer, are not the ways of reasonable men as the sequel proved. There were two things I determined at all hazards to save, firstly a door way which remained with the stone hinge intact and which I desired to be seen by one of our best archaeologists before it was disturbed ; and secondly, the beautiful pattern of the tessellated floor in the adjoining room. But unfortunately, these were the main points of attack, for to save themselves the trouble of going back two yards to the plank which had been laid for their convenience in crossing the trench, all seamed to be seized with an insane desire to batter down the poor fragment of masonry which remained of the doorway end as one clodhopper after another jumped with the force of a battering ram upon the devoted wall whose mortar had crumbled with exposure over sixteen centuries – and the stones began to reel and part from each other I thought it time to protest, and I quickly asked the worst of the gang to leave the field, but the others closed around me, and I found myself on my back in the field with half a dozen atop of me, my coat torn, my legs bruised and my ear bleeding. Gathering myself together, I

tried to save the pavement which was now attacked. The huzzas were frantic when one drunken lout after another eluded me and tore up and pocketed hands full of the tesserae but the applause reached its culminating point when one ruffian, either more drunk or foolhardy than the rest, pulled out his knife and threatened to bury it in my ribs. I ordered him off the pavement, where he had been tearing up and pocketing the dies of the beautiful central pattern. The three ringleaders were driven off from the field by their friend the publican in a trap, but I followed and, calling in the services of the constable, we proceeded to his public-house, and took down the names they gave, but either the names or addresses were false, as up to the present I have not been able to find them. – I am, & c'
JOHN STORRIE
Llantwit Major, Sept. 10
(*Western Mail 14th September 1888*)

Photograph of the mosaic showing damage. From Storrie's original notebook. (Figure 13)

Storrie's photograph (Figure 13) and original notes describe the damage inflicted on the mosaic floor.'*The circle nearest the brush and pick was the one from which the dies were stolen on the night when the disturbance took place, it had just been uncovered and I had no chance to have it either drawn or photographed, the circle was rather more than two thirds complete when found.*' The masonry door structure, a rare find, that had been subject to numerous blows resulting in its destruction was described by Storrie in a newspaper article as:

The only example of a stone pivoted door ever found in Glamorganshire was utterly destroyed.(Western Mail Thursday 20th September 1888).

An alternate version of the incident however, was published in the Western Mail on Wednesday 19th of September. The paper reproduced a letter from a Mr W.H.Evans of Bridgend, who appears to have been an impartial witness to the disturbance.

"VANDALISM RAMPANT AT LLANTWIT MAJOR"

TO THE EDITOR OF THE "WESTERN MAIL"

Sir- Mr John Storrie's letter to you, and published under the above heading teems with inaccuracies and, I am really surprised that a man of his standing and capability should be guilty of gross misrepresentation. I did not belong to the party supposed to have created these "scenes", but I am prepared to prove that not a single person there on the occasion was either "half-drunk" or "foolhardy". Nothing unusual happened until Mr Storrie attacked a man and attempted to effect his ejection in the most violent manner to say the least. The stranger, ignorant of having done any wrong, was prepared to apologise if Mr Storrie explained the circumstance which necessitated such inexplicable conduct. A scuffle ensued, whereupon both fell the ground. They

were separated for few minutes, and the man voluntarily offered to leave the field whenever his friends were prepared. Mr Storrie, however, remained unpacified, and threatened to turn all out. A similar scene, I am informed took place a few days previously under the same circumstances.-I am &c.
Bridgend Sept,17.
W.H.EVANS.
(*Western Mail 19th September 1888*)

Mr Evans's letter in response to Storrie's is of particular interest as he makes reference to a "similar scene" taking place a few days earlier. What occurred then is not documented, but perhaps Storrie was involved in a previous altercation, and with this still fresh in his mind, his temper erupted when he was confronted by a second group who acted in a manner which annoyed him during their visit. During the mid to late eighteen hundreds, the level of education of the general population was not particularity high, and thus uneducated visitors would have had little concept of an archaeological site's fragility and its preservation protocol to be observed during visits. In considering Mr Evan's account, perhaps the visiting group of men, under the influence of drink and ignorant of the site's significance and vulnerability, may have walked through the excavation causing unintentional damage. Storrie, lost his temper and the altercation erupted. Mr Evans makes no mention of the involvement of a knife, a disturbing facet of Storrie's account. It seems inconceivable that Mr Evans would write a fictitious account given that his name and address would have been supplied in order for his letter to be published. This requirement is clearly printed in the Western Mail under its Correspondence heading, '*We cannot publish any letter unless the writer sends his REAL name and ADDRESS, not necessarily for publication, but as a guarantee of good faith.*' Indeed, if a knife was involved then presumably the incident would have been judged as serious by the constabulary who would have pursued matters, with Mr Evans being called as a witness. Mr Evans's letter, effected a rapid reply from Storrie, with the Western Mail publishing his response the following day.

"VANDALISM AT LLANTWIT MAJOR"

TO THE EDITOR OF THE "WESTERN MAIL

SIR,-The above was not the terms applied by me, but by the editor of the Western Mail, to the proceedings of Monday week, but I now assert that vandalism of the worst kind was rampant on the field of Caermead on Monday week. And I think it would have been much better and fairer had both "Morien" and Mr W.H.Evans awaited the issue of the police-court proceedings before commenting on this matter in the way they have done, for, in spite of every influence that has been brought to bear this [illeg] that it must come to, as I would be [illeg](wanting?) in my duty, and utterly unfitted for the [illeg] (station?) I hold, if I assented to any compromise, in a case where the only example of a stone pivoted door ever found in Glamorganshire was utterly destroyed and the best example of a geometrical tessellated floor ever found in South Wales was wantonly damaged before my eyes, as was done on that occasion.—I am, &c.,

JOHN STORRIE.

(*Western Mail 20th September 1888*)

Storrie was a character who held strong views and was not reticent in speaking his mind, or confronting others. John Ward who succeeded Storrie as the Curator of the Cardiff Museum commented that his (Storrie's) *'pugnacity and love of controversy, frequently brought him into collision with those who differed.'* Storrie's disputes and friction with the influential members of Cardiff Society preceding the 1888 excavations, perhaps acted as a catalyst for his response to an intrusion onto the site, by a group of disruptive locals. Whatever the truth, the consequence of the incident was that the Naturalists' were faced with a visitor problem and subsequently had to arrange for a police presence (Figure 14) and an admissions charge to prevent a further reoccurrence and more damage to the site, as their meeting minutes detail.

A gatekeeper was employed to restrict access at a cost of £1-10-0, a week, and three policemen engaged to take charge of the field in turns for the sum of 30 shillings each a week, commencing duties on the 17th of September.

(Cardiff Naturalists' Society Meeting Minutes 27th September 1888)

This incident appears to have set a precedent for Storrie's subsequent excavations of the Roman villa at Ely, Cardiff some years later as revealed in the Cardiff Naturalists' Society meeting minutes of July 17th 1894. *'Resolved that the Hon.Sec write to Captain Lindsey requesting him to afford Mr Storrie the necessary police protection to the excavations.'*

The Naturalists' Society arranged a field meeting to the excavations on Friday 14th of September, with tickets for the day costing 7 shillings and 6 pence (Figure 15) and the itinerary printed in the usual Naturalists' circular (Figure 15). The journey from Cardiff to Llantwit Major took three hours and after enjoying lunch, Storrie acted as their guide, showing the work being conducted and its results. Their visit was described in some detail by the South Wales Echo.

Cardiff Naturalists at Llantwit Major Roman Remains
Yesterday the members of the Cardiff Naturalists Society paid a

Storrie? and police constable with the damaged door area in foreground. From Storrie's original notebook. At that time the Police Station in Llantwit was located at Hillhead with the local police officer being either Thomas Cole (1881 census) or John Page (1891 census). (Figure 14)

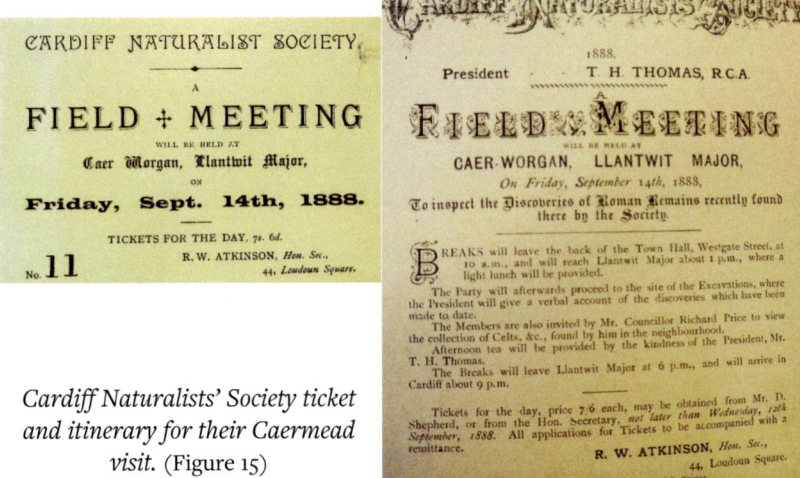

Cardiff Naturalists' Society ticket and itinerary for their Caermead visit. (Figure 15)

visit to the locality where the interesting discoveries of Roman remains have recently been made. Numbering about 50 including a few invited friends, they left Cardiff shortly after ten o'clock in three brakes, provided by Messars Hurley and Son. The drive to Llantwit Major by way of Old Post Inn and Cowbridge was of a most delightful character.

Among those present were Mr T H Thomas, Mr F A Evans and Miss Evans, Mr Layshon, Mr J Moore, Mr Boaton, Mr Gavey, Mr Daniel Rees, Mr William Davies and Mrs Davies, Mr William Lewis and Mrs Lewis, Mr H Crossley, MrJ Bell and Miss Bell, Mr T W H Plain and Miss Plain, Mrs McDonald, Mr C T Whitmell, Mr Ronnfeldt, Mr Richardson, Dr Vachell, Mr T W Proger, Mr Ivor James, Dr and Mrs De Vere Hunt, Mr Edward Hancock and Miss Hancock, Mr Loius, Mr C H James, Miss David, Miss Atkinson and Mr R W Atkinson, the honorary secretary of the society, to whose efforts much of the success of today's proceedings is due. A more charming day could not have been selected, and to many members of the party the chief attraction of the excursion lay in the relief from the entourage of the town, provided by this enjoyable drive. If, perhaps the sun was a little too hot and the dust a little too aggressive, yet there were ample palliatives to these drawbacks in the excellent hostelries which break up the journey into three stages, and when finally the party did arrive at Llantwit, they sat down to a substantial luncheon provided by Mrs Jones, of the Cross Keys Hotel. Taking the opportunity afforded by the usual post-prandial pause, Mr T H Thomas, R.C.A, president of the society informed those present that the chief object of that day's outing was to show the members of the society and others interested in antiquarian and archaeological researches now being pursued in the district, that the affair was really of a very important nature. Of course funds were required to prosecute this work, and the secretary would be very glad to receive subscriptions *towards that end. He might add that from what he had heard during the visit of the British Association to Bath, that a donation would probably be voted in their aid, to enable the explorations to be carried out systematically and fully. The party then proceeded across the fields from Llantwit to the site of the excavations, which have been conducted in a field about a mile distant from the village. A full description of the discoveries has already appeared in these columns, and there is now little doubt that the opinion then advanced to the effect that the site of Bovium has been discovered is correct. Mr Storrie, who is still actively engaged in the work of excavation, acted as a guide to the visitors, and throughly explained the nature of the undertaking and demonstrated the results. The principle item of interest was the square room with its tessellated pavement, some portions of which are intact revealing a very beautiful pattern. In this chamber and an adjoining room 41 skeletons have a been discovered, together with the remains of two horses. All the skeletons have had their skull fractured, and it is presumed that this place was the scene of a massacre by the Irish in A.D 466, when they overran the country during one of their periodic invasions. The marks of the horses hoofs are quite visible on the delicate mosaic, and from the fact that four of the skeletons are interned in roughly constructed graves in the floor, it would seam that the invaders buried their own dead, but left the other corpses as they fell. It is a matter of current belief that St Patrick[3], the patron saint of Ireland was taken prisoner here when a youth and sent as a slave to the sister isle, so that the event may have occurred during that very incursion of the barbarians of which the terrible record has now been laid bare after a lapse of fourteen centuries. There was much learned discussion, and equally learned differences of opinion amongst those who viewed the remains, but everyone agreed as to their importance and interest. Some excitement has been imported*

into the explorations by the fact that Mr Storrie has had to defend his treasures vi et armis against some modern Vandals. Last Sunday some enterprising excursionists visited the place, and commenced to dig up the marble squares which comprise the pavement. When remonstrated with by Mr Storrie they ill-treated him with some violence and succeeded in destroying about two square feet of the mosaic before they left. This act was one of sheer and wanton ignorance, combined with brutality, and it is a pity that the offenders cannot be punished. When tired of the Roman remains the party returned to Llantwit, and examined the old church and it's romantic surroundings, finally leaving the pleasant little village about 5.30 p.m. They stopped at the Bear Hotel, Cowbridge where by the courtesy of the president, an excellent tea was partaken of, and thenceforth the run home was most pleasant. Cardiff was reached before 9 p.m.'
(South Wales Echo September 15th 1888)

Chapter 3

The Villa Revealed

Storrie's excavation trench in the field was to eventually extend to around 290 feet in length and approximately 5 feet in width. He was careful to ensure that the trench was excavated along its length to a sufficient depth to unearth all likely remains. '*I carried it down everywhere till I came to the undisturbed ground, whatever the depth might be.*' His modus operandi was to trench in the chosen direction, branching outwards whenever an area of interest was found. By this means he was able to construct a plan of the excavation showing the rooms unearthed and detailing finds made along its length (Figure 16). By September the excavations were in the process of completion for that season, with the trench reaching its furthest western extent. Here, a room containing a hypocaust was uncovered. Immediately outside the western wall of this room, a large quantity of floor tiles were present and on its adjoining northern wall an opening was discovered at base level. This orifice was thought to have housed a furnace acting as a heat source for the room. In a later lecture on the excavations at Cardiff University to the Naturalists' Society, Storrie suggested that this room could have provided two functions. '*Further on were found remains either of a bath roughly formed or of an arrangement for heating a living room.*' (*Western Mail 13th October, 1888*). This was the last room to be described in his notes and his subsequent publication for the Cardiff Naturalists'. The Cardiff Times, publishing an extensive report on the excavations, describes this room as considerably grander than the evidence indicated and speculated on the whole structure being a Roman town.

At the further end of the trench, where the most recent excavations have been carried on, is a large Roman bath, which, from its size and the nature of its accessories in the way of heating appliances, (sic) &c., cannot have been intended for a private residence, but has evidently been of a public character.

A trench 410 feet long, averaging three feet wide and running from two to eight feet in depth.

Extending along its entire length are the walls and floor of houses built in the Roman style of architecture.

The explorers may have hit upon the exact site of Bovium, a Roman town, which is marked on the maps of England of that period in that neighbourhood.

On many of the walls are traces of fire, and it would seem that the place was destroyed by a hostile force.
(Cardiff Times September 1st 1888)

In reality, Storrie had partly excavated the northernmost remains of a single large Roman villa, rather than a number of individual houses, and certainly not a whole town or the elusive Bovium. Finds along the length of the excavation included worked stone (querns), iron (both unworked and finished products), bronze products, fragments of glass, Roman coins, pottery fragments, organic remains such as shellfish (notably oyster), animal and human bones, skeletons and considerable quantities of charcoal. It was the charcoal, distributed along the length of the excavation, together with the human and horse remains that prompted Storrie to propose a violent end to the villa. In his original notes under the heading Fire he wrote '*Nothing can be more evident than that the whole place has been burnt down as everywhere charcoal was found, the nails of the*

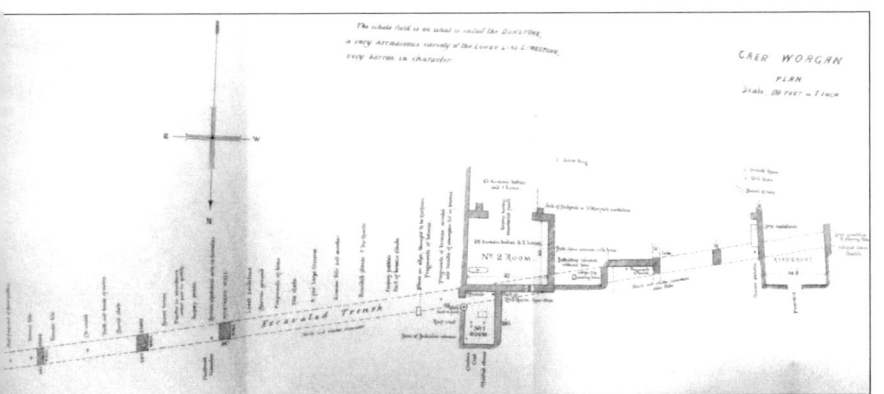

Storrie's plan of the site. After Storrie, J. (1888) Cardiff Naturalists' Society Report and Transactions, Vol. XX, Part II, p. 49.) (Figure 16)

slates and the larger ones that held the rafters together were twisted and bent from the action of fire, the stones were burnt red and the roof slates were burnt red nearly through.'

From the positions of the skeletons in Room 2, (Figure 8) Storrie conjectured that they might have been the Romano-British occupants of the villa. He assumed that these unfortunate residents had been massacred, plundered and left where they fell, by Irish pirates, who were believed to have raided the coastal areas during the early fifth century CE. He thought that the carbon deposits unearthed suggested the burning of the villa during a raid, adding plausibility to his supposition. The crudely buried skeletons he considered to be of a larger race due to their longer skulls, and were the conquerors who, having died during their raid were then buried by their comrades. He did note however that no trace of any weapons, or parts of such, were found, a detail that apportioned uncertainty to his hypothesis. In recent work (2004) using Accelerator Mass Spectrometry, Dr Alice Roberts has shown that the skeletal remains at the villa date from approximately 640-670 CE and 790-990 CE constituting an early medieval cemetery overlying the villa. The use of villas at the end of the Roman period as cemeteries was very common in France and Belgium, where hundreds of examples exist, although in Britain the practice appears to have been less frequent. On the continent there are a number of examples where burials are found in an orderly fashion inside villa rooms. At Berthelming Villa, Moselle there are twenty four burials in the room corners in rudimentary coffins, and at Pompogne, Lot-et-Garonne a seventh and eighth century CE cemetery overlays a series of mosaic pavements. At the Llantwit villa, the most probable explanation is that when the villa was abandoned it was used as a rudimentary cemetery in the period before the establishment of the twelfth century monastery near the present day site of St Illtud's[1] church.

By late September the exposed structures were being prepared for re-covering (Figure 17) to afford protection during the approaching winter, and the local press were announcing the ending of visiting opportunities.

The Excavations at Llantwit Major

We are informed that the excavations near Llantwit Major will be left open for public view for a short time longer, but they must be covered over before the appearance of the first frost, as no further steps can be taken this season to complete the explorations. An admission fee, however will be charged to defray the expense of the constables watching the neighbourhood.
(*Western Mail September 22nd 1888*)

The minutes of the Cardiff Naturalists' Society meeting of the 27th September, provide details of the costs incurred and monies received in respect of the excavations. During the time the field had been open to the public from the 17th to the 24th of September a charge of 6 pence per person entering had been levied, producing a total of £13 12s 0d which equated to five hundred and forty four paying visitors. Each evening the gatekeeper handed the revenue collected to Mr G.W.Nicholl, a prominent member of the local community. Up to the 27th of September the total costs inclusive of the policemen and gatekeeper had been £23 14s 06d. Subscriptions had been paid or promised to the total of £28 08s 0d, from the following:-

Cardiff Naturalist's Society £10, The Library and Museum Committee £10, Col. J. Picton Turberville £4 12s 6d, Mr O.H.Jones £ 1, Mr J.J.Neale 10s 6d, Morgannwg £1, Mr C.J.Whitwell 10s, Mr Geo. Grove 10s and Mr C.H.James 5s.

Also, at this meeting it was resolved that the site be closed to the public on the 13th of October and that Storrie would be requested to commence filling in of the exposed remains on Monday 15th, with an express instruction to prevent any damage to the tessellated pavement. Subsequent excavation of the site (1938-1948) by Dr V.E.Nash-Williams commended Storrie's preservation, especially that of the mosaic pavement, which had been carefully edged with cement and boarded over, before covering. Awareness of this conservation had also disseminated to local inhabitants, as recorded by Professor William Davies some four decades later. *'When excavations at Caer Mead (sic) were filed in, a covering of wood, on which concrete was superimposed, was placed over the mosaic.' (The letters of Professor William Davies [Papers in L.M.L.H.S.Archive]. Facts Gathered from a Conversation with Mr Frank Davies, Aged C 65 Sept 1930 [Uncle].)*

Not withstanding the unfortunate incident by the group of local males, the majority of visits appeared to be trouble free and included prominent academics, and interested members of the local aristocracy. Certainly, in the last week or so of the excavation, aristocracy were prominent in their visits, with the Duke and Duchess of Teck's[2] visit to Dunraven and subsequently Caermead being widely reported in the local press.

Royal Visit to Dunraven
Next Saturday the Duchess of Teck (Princess Mary of Cambridge) will pay a visit to the Earl and Countess of Dunraven. The Dutchess will arrive by afternoon express. The townsfolk of Bridgend intend to make a demonstration on the occasions, and the town will be decorated.
(South Wales Echo September 17th 1888)

Following this article, the Western Mail of 24th of September 1888, recounts their visit to Bridgend in great detail, apportioning considerable space and sketches to describe their arrival and the reception. Whilst staying at Dunraven, they no doubt came to hear of the excavation work at Caermead and a visit was duly arranged as reported in the South Wales Daily News of September the 26th in its update on the progress at the site.

The Roman Remains at Llantwit
Mr Storrie took some photographs of the interesting discoveries at Llantwit Major on Tuesday, and the Duke and Dutchess of Teck were expected to visit the scene of operations in the afternoon. The public will not have an opportunity of visiting Caerwrgan (sic) after this week, as steps will be taken to cover over the chambers on Monday. This is necessary to preserve the remains from rain and frost. It is intended, if arrangements can be made, to pursue the excavations next year, as the outlines of eleven more chambers which form a quadrangle have been defined.

The visit actually took place on the 1st of October 1888, as referred to in the Glamorgan Gazette article from June 3rd 1910 below. Unfortunately the visitors book mentioned in the article can no longer be located.

Local Gossip
The reference to Queen Mary's visit ...Princess to Dunraven Castle reminded Mr Ward, the curator of the Welsh Museum at Cardiff, that during that visit she inspected the Roman remains which were then being excavated at Caerwrgan, (sic) near Llantwit Major. Upon going through the visitors book used at the excavations he found her signature under date October 1st 1888, with those of the Duke and Dutchess of Teck and of the Countess of Dunraven and her daughters. The young Princess signed herself "Victoria Mary of Teck" in a clear and firm hand. As her signature will, doubtless, interest many, the book is placed opened at the page in one of the glass cases of the first antiquities room in the museum; and the same page is also distinguished by the signature, on the day following, of the late Lieutenant-General Pitt-Rivers, F.R.S., inspector of ancient monuments, and one of our most distinguished archaeologists.

Another distinguished visitor and supporter of the project was Lord Bute, (John Patrick Crichton-Stuart 3rd Marquess of Bute 1847-1900). Lord Bute, accompanied by Mr James Corbett, paid a visit to the site on the afternoon of Saturday 29th of September, when they were greeted by Storrie, Dr P.Rhys Griffiths and Professors Parker and Thomas of the University College of South Wales (now Cardiff University). The newspapers described how Bute, in company with Storrie, minutely examined the progress of the work. After Bute's departure, Dr Griffiths and both professors, continued their work, and before darkness descended they succeeded in exhuming a complete skeleton of a forty year old male in a good state of preservation.

The Roman Remains at Llantwit Major
Visit of Lord Bute to Caerwrgan (sic)

On Saturday the Marquis of Bute accompanied by Mr Corbett, visited the field at Caer Wrgan, near Llantwit Major, where Cardiff Naturalists' Society has recently made the important discoveries of Roman antiquities leading to the belief that the exact site of Bomium has been found. Mr Storrie, curator to the Cardiff Museum, received his lordship (who drove from Llantrissant), and explained to him all the operations that have been conducted during the past two months, with the results already described in these columns. Lord Bute took the greatest interest in the excavation, and expressed the hope that the Cardiff Naturalists' Society would continue their explorations until the ground had been throughly exhausted, and its hidden reminiscences of a past age laid bare. Their researches he remarked, could not fail to prove very valuable to antiquaries and archaeologists. During the afternoon Mr T.H.Thomas, R.C.A., president of the society and Dr Rhys Griffiths visited the spot with the object of removing some of the skeletons for careful scientific examination, particularly with regard to measurements of bones etc, as the facts thus deduced may prove of anthropological interest. In a short period the works will be covered with earth for the winter.
(South Wales Daily News 1st October 1888 (Swansea Edition)

Sometime after Bute's visit the excavations were reburied by Storrie and his accomplices, and the site was to remain closed until the late 1930's, despite Bute's hope that the Cardiff Naturalists' would continue the project. In their meeting of the 17th of October 1888 the Naturalists' were informed by Dr Vachell that obtaining a lease of the ground had made little progress and their existing one, obtained by Storrie, was due for expiry in February 1889. At this point they were also beginning to explore the publishing of a report on the project and this task was allocated to the editing committee. The costs of the project were detailed in the meeting of the 6th of November when Lord Bute was thanked for his contribution of £7-13-06, in payment for the cementing (Figure 17) and preservation the tessellated pavement before re-covering.

Date	Payments		Receipts	
1888. Aug 22nd	Paid Mr Storrie	5-0-0	Subscriptions	1-2-6
	? Repaid	1-25		1-5-6
		3-17-7		10-6
1888. Aug 31st	Paid Mr Storrie	5.		4-12-6
	Dr Vachell	2.		7-10-6
1888. Sept 13th	Mr Storrie	5.	Gate Money	33-10-6
15th	Mr Storrie	4-10-0	Lord Bute	7-13-6
22nd	Mr Storrie	3-9-6	The Library Committee	
				10-0-0
	Rent of field	8-0-0		
	Gate keeper	3-3-0		
	Cementing	7-13-6		
	Board and lodging	2-5-0		
	Hire and Materials	2-6-9		
	Wages	9-9-0		
	Balance in hand	2-0-2		
		£58-14-6		£58-14-6

At this meeting the publishing of an account of the exploration was discussed and a sum not exceeding twenty five pounds was agreed to be spent. A sub-committee consisting of Mr Thomas, Dr Vachell, Mr Corbett, Mr Storrie and the Hon.Sec, was formed to to make the necessary arrangements. The same evening, during a following-on meeting of the Caer Worgan (sic) subcommittee, Storrie handed in his report together with a note on the origins of the name Caer Worgan[3]. It was decided to send the report, in turn to each member of the sub-committee, and to arrange for the plan of the site to be lithographed by a Mr Tilley. The tessellated pavement was a significant find, and Vachell undertook to liaise with Dr B. Redwood about the use of the "stones" he was having prepared to produce a lithograph of it. Lithographs were produced by drawing a copy of the image with a wax substance on to a smooth limestone surface, sometimes termed "stones". The surface was then treated with acid and gum arabic which etched the portions of the limestone that were not protected by the wax, thus producing a copy of the design. By applying ink to the surface, copies of the original image could be transferred to paper. The meeting also decided to select various objects unearthed during the excavations for Mr T.H.Thomas to prepare illustrations, and General Pitt Rivers[4] was tasked with the examination and preparation of illustrations of the human remains.

At the following meeting of the 16th of November, Dr

Securing of the mosaic with a cement edging.
From Storrie's original notebook. (Figure 17)

Vachell informed the committee that Mr Nicholl had made a beautiful drawing of the tessellated pavement (Figure 18) which the Society was free to use, and suggested that it be engraved and copies coloured by hand. By March the publication was making progress, and it was agreed to include twelve pages of text and two lithographs in the Societies Transactions, Volume XX part two. In April the committee meeting agreed to send an advance copy of the Llantwit report to the Cambrian Archaeological Association, with a note to the effect that the report had not yet been issued to the members. Three zinc blocks detailing views of the excavations, were offered by Mr Thomas to the Naturalists' to produce figures for Report. Two hundred and fifty extra copies of the Llantwit pavement drawing were authorised to be printed at a cost of £1 7s 6d on superior paper. The Committee agreed to pay Mr J.Tilley £3 7s 6d for the lithographs. In July, the Committee resolved to

Tesselated pavement drawing attributed to Illtyd Nicholl. After Storrie, J. (1888) Cardiff Naturalists' Society Report and Transactions, Vol. XX, Part II, p.49. (Figure 18)

supply a messrs J.W. Lewis copies of the pavement (mosaic) which had been hand coloured for general sale at a cost of 2 s 6 d each, and in the September meeting that Mr Illtyd Nicholl be presented with fifty copies printed on superior paper. Problems however arose with the pavement drawing as revealed by the minutes of the Naturalists' meetings of the 27th of November and the 4th of December 1888.

The Hon.Sec. explained that he had written to Mr Illtyd Nicholl respecting the assignment of the copyright of the drawing of the Llantwit Major pavement, but that he had received no reply. He was instructed to write again to Mr Nicholl.'

'The Hon. Sec. was requested to write to Mr Nicholl informing him that the Society had no intention of depriving him of the power of presenting a selling for local charities the drawing of the Llantwit pavement and they suggested the copyright should be a joint one.'

Storrie's report was published in the Transactions of the Cardiff Naturalists' Society, *'Report and Transactions'* 1888, Vol. XX, Part II, pp. 49-61, (Figure 19) and includes a plan of the villa, illustrations of the excavation trench, the pinnacle, burial urn and plaster remains found. The drawing of the tessellated pavement by Mr Nicholl is absent from this publication, but a drawing of the pavement is present, as a folded monochromatic insert in the separate published copies of the report. This drawing remains unattributed in the report, but is possibly the one by Nicholl that Dr Vachell alluded to in the Naturalists' meeting of the 16th of November. Storrie's work during the summer of 1888 had only excavated a small portion of the villa, and from his survey of the whole site, he knew that much more of this extensive structure remained to be uncovered. The Cardiff Naturalists' also echoed Bute's sentiment, with plans for a return the following summer, and indeed Storrie refers to further exploration in his lecture to the Naturalists' in October 1888.

> *The remains, Mr Storrie said, would be completely filled in in a few days, and he hoped that next year the excavations would be continued.*
> (*Western Mail* 13th October 1888)

The possibility of further excavations revealing additional information about this major Roman site in South Wales had not just attracted widespread attention locally, but had also reached a wider audience. The Inspector of Ancient Monuments in Britain, Lieutent-General A.Pitt Rivers, in a letter to the editor of the Times of Monday 2nd June 1890, entitled 'Wanted, An English Exploration Fund' uses a reference to the Roman Villa at Llantwit Major, along with other examples to support his proposition. '*As showing promise to be one of the most interesting in Britain, and which is the only existing one in South Wales.*' In 1891, the British Association's week long meeting, which commenced in Cardiff on Wednesday 19th, August, lists an excursion to Caermead. '*to the remains of the Roman Villa at Llantwit Major (discovered a year or two ago).(Birmingham Daily Post Monday 17th August 1891).*

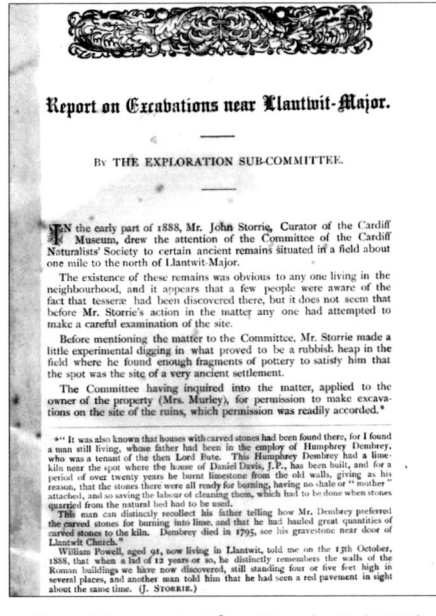

Storrie's report. After Storrie, J. (1888) Cardiff Naturalists' Society Report and Transactions, Vol. XX, Part II, p. 49.
(Figure 19)

Unfortunately, no further excavations were performed in the immediate years on such a promising site for which great expectations existed to reveal a wealth of knowledge of the Romanisation of South Wales. Storrie's notes strongly suggest that the reason for this was due to an undercurrent of discontentment by the owners of Caermead, towards him personally. In one paragraph he adds a subtle defence of himself portraying the owners as the uncompromising party responsible for further work being negated.

What was the cause of you being stopped from continuing the excavation is frequently asked and in reply I can only say that I am not able to say, as I did not at the time or at any time since perceive any reason further than it was the wish of the owners that the excavations should be closed up and the field returned to its original state, and although various excuses have reached me, they have been extremely trivial in nature, as to be unworthy of notice. Thinking that possibly, the reason might be a personal dislike to myself I stood aside but none of those gentlemen who have attempted to reopen the matter seem to have been more successful than myself.

However, another facet of the affair, carries more substance as the primary reason for the cessation of work after only one season. Mr Corbett had been the representative of the Cardiff Naturalists' in communicating with Mrs Murley's solicitors to arrange a lease of the ground. As detailed in the Naturalists' minutes of the meeting of 9th of January 1889, a lease was in preparation, but on assignment, the field would need a significant amount of money apportioned to it in order to further the work.

Dr Vachell mentioned that negotiations were in progress in obtaining a lease of the field, Caer Mead (sic), and said that when the preparation of the lease was complete an amount of money, about £600, would have to be spent upon it for the purpose of putting up, building fences etc, and under the circumstances he asked for an expression of opinion as to whether the Committee would undertake to carry out the work, or would prefer to leave it to a larger & independent Committee upon which the Society would be represented.

The following resolution was proposed by Major E.R.Jones, seconded by Mr W. Ronnfeldt and carried unanimously. Resolved that "while heartily approving of the measures taken by Dr Vachell in securing the field at Llantwit with a view to further excavations, this Society regrets that it is not financially in a position to undertake the work itself.'

With the Naturalists' unable to commit funds to lease and physically enclose Caermead, to continue excavations, the site would remain destined to be undisturbed in the following decades. For Storrie however, the personalities of those involved, still remained the foremost reason for the closure and abandonment of the site. During a British Archaeological Association visit to the Vale of Glamorgan on Friday 26th of August 1892 the members focused on the church and Celtic stones at Llantwit Major, before concluding their excursion with a presentation of papers at Barry. Storrie presented a paper entitled *"The Roman Villa at Llantwit Major"* in which he makes no reference to the financial aspect, only a thinly veiled accusation against the landowners and locals who had caused problems and damage, directly resulting in the cessation of his work. The Western Mail of Saturday 27th of August 1892 reported the visit and reproduced Storrie's pointed remarks.'*Mr Storrie expressed great regret that the excavations at this exceptionally historic place had been repeatedly interfered with.'*

In the following years, one other member of the academic community expressed a more optimistic outlook, although the fiscal problem would have still been casting a shadow over the enterprise. Mr John Ward, the then Curator of Cardiff Museum remained hopeful about the possibility of further excavations to expand on Storrie's limited work.

> *The excavation was only partial, but quite sufficient to show that the site was of no mean Roman villa. It is to be hoped that the work will be resumed, for if it is conducted again with the same care, it cannot fail to throw abundant light on Roman provincial life.*
> *The Antiquary* (1893) Vol. XXVI, pp. 51-58

At the beginning of the twentieth century, Ernest Vachell, the son of Ellen Murley from her fist marriage to Frederick Charles Vachell, had plans to re-excavate the site and display the artefacts recovered in Llantwit Major Town Hall.

Mr Vatchell[5] (sic) (Mrs E. T. Lloyd's former husband) had it in mind just before he died to re-excavate Caer Mead (sic) & place all the relics discovered in a room under the Town Hall.
(The letters of Professor William Davies: Facts Gathered from a Conversation with Mr Frank Davies, Aged C 65 Sept 1930 [Uncle], Papers in L.M.L.H.S.Archive.)

Despite the plans of people such as these, Storrie's work was to remain the only intrusion into the remains until the late 1930's. Notwithstanding that Storrie's excavations were confined to a few rooms comprising the northern part of the villa, he had during his limited work uncovered revealing details of is structure, size and history. His trenching had revealed a construction of some quality, with substantial stone walls coated with painted plasterwork on the interior, and a roof of pennant sandstone, with one section finished with an ornate Bath Stone finial and ridge. The pennant roof slates were mostly octagonal in shape, although a few pentagonal samples were uncovered. They were attached to the roof by means of nails through a hole in one corner (Figure 20), and Storrie's notes state that a few examples remained with the original nails still in situ. The mosaic pavement, augmented by the hypocaust room added to the aura of elegance of the residential section and hinted at an owner of some importance. In contrast to this opulence, his findings in Room 1 had shown that the villa also possessed an artisan aspect, imparted by evidence of metal smelting indicating the presence of workers, possibly resident as villa staff. The everyday life of the occupants was revealed by the discovery of pottery of varying types and dietary detritus, such as marine species, deer and swine. Farm stock including sheep and cattle hinted at the villa's animal husbandry and fiscal aspects were suggested by numerous Roman coinage of various emperors. At the conclusion of the excavations, Storrie must have been aware, that notwithstanding the size of the villa, it would hardly constitute a Roman town and thus the much sought site of Bovium would still remain elusive. However, its size would have stimulated conjecture on its proximity to an avenue of movement, since the output of crops and livestock would require easy transport to the nearest market town. Although in his notes, Storrie makes no mention of any definite access or road to the villa, an interesting article in the Athenaeum publication by Mr W. E.Winks, Honorary Curator, Cardiff Museum, mentions the investigation of a Roman road from what he terms Caer Wrgan (sic) leading westward.

While these excavations have been going on, special attention has been called to the traces of a Roman road leading from this site—Caer Wrgan (sic)—-to another site of no small interest called locally Tre Wrgan, (sic) half a mile away to the west. That a connextion (sic) must have existed between Wrgan's Castle

Photograph of sandstone roof slate showing nail hole; bottom right of photograph. From Storrie's original notebook. (Figure 20)

> *and Wrgans Town is evident, if only from the fact that the well which afforded their common water supply lies halfway between the two places. It now transpires that when the house called "The Downs" was built on the site of Tre Wrgan, twenty seven years ago, the workmen, in digging for foundations, came upon remains which, judging by the account given of them, must have been Roman. It is a matter of deep regret that no proper notice was taken of these discoveries at the time when they were made.*
> (*The Athenaeum* 20th October 1888)

Winks further speculates that the road from Caer Wrgan to Tre-Wrgan was part of a Via Martimia, a connecting road which supposition considered, ran from the Via Julia through Bovium to the coast. The existence of a connecting road is also mentioned by Professor William Davies in his typewritten notes, Llantwit and its Past *'It is interesting to note that old*

"Roman" foundations are said to have been found when building the Downs Farm, which is still connected to Cae Mead (sic) by a disused roadway.' (Professor Davies Papers Papers in L.M.L.H.S.Archive.)
A geo-physical survey conducted in 2016 by Cardiff University, found evidence of a possible Early Medieval period track that led to the north of the site, from the west, but no significant evidence of a road directly entering the villa complex itself. The track in question may well have followed the boundary which now forms the modern day northern hedge of Caermead field past the spring of Fynnon Caermead[6], and through the current railway line. Today, a narrow lane exists to the west of the railway line that eventually opens onto the modern road near the Downs. Therefore, the possibility exists, that during the centuries of the Roman era the villa was connected to the Downs in the west along this track (Figure 3).

Although Storrie was unable to revisit the site to conduct further excavations he did return to Llantwit Major to present his findings at a public lecture at the Town Hall in some years later on the 8th of March 1895.

> *Llantwit Major*
> *LECTURE.—Mr John Storrie (late curator of Cardiff Museum), gave a lecture at the Town Hall on Friday, the 8th inst. The lecture consisted of original views of the Roman remains at Cardiff Ely Racecourse, and Llantwit Major. The lecture throughout was very interesting, especially that part bearing on Llantwit, the "find" at Caerwrgan (sic) still being fresh in most people's minds. The attendance was fairly good.*
> *(Glamorgan Gazette 15th March 1895)*

Chapter 4

The 1933 Attempt to Re-open the Villa Site

Unfortunately, despite the academic community's optimism in the immediate years after 1888, a renewed excavation remained elusive and the field reverted to its former use as pasture, serving grazing livestock. Even after lying undisturbed for some forty five years, the villa had not been forgotten, and there appears to have been an impetus in the local community to resurrect its prominence. During the Parish Council meeting of the 27th of June 1933, Mr L.G.Grey, the local pharmacy owner proposed that an effort should be made to obtain the interest of the Archaeological Society, with a view to preserving the historical monuments in the parish, in particular the re-excavation of the Roman Villa at Caermead. He suggested that the Clerk, Mr Samuel Allen *'communicate with some responsible authority and point out the desire of the Council in this direction.'* Mr Illtyd Andrews, (the brother of the local postmaster and previous Town Clerk Mr Hughie Andrews) seconded the motion which was accepted. It is unclear what Archaeological Society Mr Grey was referring to as the only record of a Llantwit Major Archaeology Society was a society formed in 1936, as detailed in the diary of Hughie Andrews. *'Sept 14 – Willie Davies and Sid Havard came in tonight (the post office in L/M). We decided to form a local Archaeological Society.'*

His diary entry on November 3rd mentioned a report of the formation of the archaeological society in a newspaper article, but he failed to record its source (research identified it as the Glamorgan Gazette).

A meeting of the local Archaeological Society was held at the Post Office on Monday evening, Mr H.Andrews and Mr S.Hafod (sic) [Havard] acting in the capacities of chairman and secretary respectively. Many items concerning the Society were discussed. The officials are anxious to extend this interesting past-time, which will thrive on excavations in such an old, historic area as Llantwit and the surrounding district. Among others present were Messer's P.C.Fisher and W.H.Davies M.A.

An illustrated lecture having bearing on the Society was given at St. Illtud's Church on Tuesday evening by Mr V.E.Nash Williams M.A. F.S.A., of the Cardiff Museum, his subject being The Celtic Church in Wales and Ireland.
(Glamorgan Gazette 11th December 1936)

Perhaps, in 1933 Mr Grey was referring to an existing scholarly body such as the Cambrian Archaeological Association or the reference was to the Archaeology Department at the National Museum of Wales. As a consequence of his proposal, on 30th June 1933, Mr Allen, wrote a letter to the Director of the National Museum of Wales, Cardiff, Dr Cyril Fox indicating that the Parish Council was keen to renew excavations at Caermead.

Dear Sir,

I am instructed by the Parish Council to bring to your notice that there is a general desire on the part of the inhabitants that some steps be taken to preserve places of historical interest in the parish.

Llantwit Major is, of course, teeming with items of interest to antiquarians and the present generation deplore the fact that excavations of the Roman Villa of Caer Mead (sic) in 1888, which yielded so many historical treasures, were filled in after a brief interval.

The Council is of the opinion that this spot, particularly, is

worthy of being once more excavated and I ask if you would kindly give the council the benefit of your experience as to the best method of obtaining the interest of any society that would be likely to give this their consideration.
Thanking you in anticipation,
Yours faithfully,
Sam Allen
Clerk to the Parish Council.

The minutes of the Parish Council for July, record that Mr Allen had written to the museum after consultation with a Mr Loveluck and that the Museum had replied in the first instance to indicate that Dr Fox was on holiday, but that he would be made aware of their communication on his return. In a reply of 11th of August, Dr Fox states that he would be very interested in the proposal, citing that the villa was well-known and should be subject to an adequate investigation. In the first instance he cautioned that the co-operation of the owner would need to be obtained, to place the site at the disposal of competent excavators for a reasonable period. In response, Mr Allen confirmed that the matter would be scheduled for the next meeting of the Parish Council on the 29th of August. At this meeting Mr Allen informed the Council that he had entered into correspondence on the 18th of August with the site owner, Mr Albert A. Doughty, a butcher of Barry and Llantwit Major who had purchased Caermead for two thousand pounds in 1919. The land at Caermead bought by Mr Doughty was one of forty eight lots in a sale catalogue of 1919, (the Vachell Sale Catalogue) which disposed of land belonging to the remaining Wilkins/Vachell beneficiaries, Isidore Vachell of Folkestone and Benjamin Lampard-Vachell, of Surrey. Both brothers no longer had any association with the Llantwit Major area, and their disposal of properties and land in the Llantwit Parish returned in excess of thirty three thousand pounds. The sale took place at the Park Hotel, Cardiff on Thursday 18th of September at 3pm under the auspices of Messrs Gottwaltz and Perry, auctioneers. Caermead, Lot 19 totalled 12.817 acres and was described as freehold meadow land, formerly the site of a Roman Villa the remains of which were exposed in 1887 and visited by H.M. the present Queen (a reference to the 1888 visit of Princess May of Teck during Storrie's excavations). The disposal of Caermead returned two thousand pounds, whilst Albert Doughty, an active buyer on the day also purchased Lot 39, 8.8 acres, let with Little Frampton for four hundred and twenty five pounds and Lot 42, 15.2 acres, close to Caermead for one thousand pounds. Doughty, resident at Morfa House at that time, is described in the house and Caermead title deeds as a shipping butcher or shipping purveyor, of Barry Docks. He therefore must have been the owner of a successful business in order to outlay £3,425 at the auction. By the 1930's he had moved to Barry, where he was contacted by Samuel Allen.

In his correspondence to Doughty, on the 18th of August, Mr Allen suggests that the villa site be subject to an excavation *'to reveal to humanity the interior, also relics of the past.'* Mr Doughty, who was at this time residing at Morfa, Romily Park Avenue, Barry replied in a prompt manner the next day stating that he was in favour of the re-opening of the site, but he would conduct the negotiations with the National Museum's officials personally. On receipt of this information, from Samuel Allen, Dr Fox, no doubt experienced in such situations, diplomatically suggests that the Parish Council should be the mediators in the proposal and the Museum would proceed once these had been adequately concluded.

Dear Sir,
I thank you for your letter of 31st August enclosing the letter of the 19th of August, 1933, which you received from Mr Albert A.

> *Doughty regarding the Roman Villa site at Caermead, Llantwit Major, which I now return.*
>
> *The invitation in this matter comes from your Parish Council which quite properly is interesting itself in place of historic interest within its area. It is clear, therefore, that all negotiations regarding the site should be dealt with by your Parish Council. As soon as these have been settled I shall be only too pleased to offer suggestions and give any advice in my power regarding the actual work of excavation.*
>
> *If, in the meantime, you would like to consult me on the matter I shall be only too ready to give you an appointment,*
> *Yours faithfully,*
> *Director.*
> *(Letter from Cyril Fox 5th of September to the Llantwit Parish Council)*

At the Council meeting of 26th of September it was resolved that an approach to Mr Doughty be made, to propose Dr Fox's suggestion that site be opened for examination by competent excavators for a suitable period of time. By the next Council meeting of 31st of October, no written response had been received from Mr Doughty. Mr Leonard Grey, however, stated that from a conversation he had with Doughty it was apparent that, although Doughty was willing for the site to be excavated it would be not without some monetary consideration to himself. Consequently, the Parish Council took the view that this was unacceptable, and that they were not able to proceed with the project in the circumstances. The situation was outlined to Cyril Fox in a letter of 3rd of November, together with a message of thanks from the Parish Council for his interest shown in the proposition. His reply, validates the sound rational for his hesitance in corresponding with Doughty on a personal level.

'Dear Mr Allen,
Roman Villa Site at Caermead
Thank you very much for your letter of the 3rd November.
I much regret that the scheme has foundered on the financial rock. This was the reason for my disinclination to make any move in the matter until I had had the definite offer of the site.

May I say that it seems to be greatly to the credit of a public body such as yours that it should take such a keen interest in research. It may be possible, on some future occasion, to reopen the question which has been discussed between us.
Believe me,
Yours very faithfully,
Director.
(Cyril Fox 4th November 1933)

Thus on two occasions, the villa which had piqued the imagination of the academic and local communities continued to conceal its narrative with access being negated by financial constraints. In 1938 however, Caermead once again became a focus of attention for archaeologists, although, on this occasion the completion of excavations would be hindered, albeit not by the landowners, or fiscal matters but this time, by the outbreak of World War Two.

Chapter 5

The 1938–1948 Excavations

In the summer of 1938 Dr Victor Erle Nash-Williams (1897-1955) (Figure 21), Keeper of the Department of Archaeology, National Museum of Wales and Lecturer in Archaeology at University College, Cardiff (now Cardiff University) began excavating at Caermead. This was to be the first of three seasons work extending over the summers of 1938, 1939 and 1940. It transpired that the third season's work had to be deferred due to the intervention of the Second World War from 1939 to 1945, and consequently the project could not be completed until the summer of 1948. Nash-Williams already had local connections through the recently formed Llantwit Major Archaeological Society, which had been founded by Prof. W. (Will) H. Davies, W. Lewis, E. H. Parry, H. Andrews and Sydney. G. Havard in 1936, (Figure 22) as previously mentioned. It is entirely possible that this group of luminaries were instrumental in instigating his subsequent interest in excavating local sites. Although no locations were referred to by name, the Glamorgan Gazette published a paragraph in its 4th of December 1936 edition, alluding to future excavations in the area. '*The local Archaeological Society under Mr Nash-Williams, of the Cardiff Museum, hopes to start excavation work in the district next summer.*' In that summer of 1937, Nash-Williams undertook an excavation of the Bishops Field adjacent to St Illtud's church, where previous unearthing had revealed the remains of a thirteenth century monastery. During this enterprise, attention turned to Caermead as a proposition for

Dr V.E. Nash-Williams. (Figure 21)

Prof. W.H. Davies

Photographs of some of the Llantwit (Illtud) Archaeological Society members on the steps of the Gate House, Llantwit dated 4/6/1937. There were five in the group so someone had to take the photograph, hence the need for two photos to record all the group members present. In the photograph are: Prof. W. (Will) H. Davies, W. Lewis, E. H. Parry, H. Andrews & , S. G. Havard. (Figure 22) excavation the following year. On the 26th of July 1937, Prof Davies wrote to the owner of Caermead, a Mr W.T.Jones of "Firs", Merthyr Dyfan Road, Bridgend, to seek his permission to undertake an investigation of the field. In his reply of the 27th Mr Jones's solicitor, Martin C.Verity of Bridgend, confirms that permission would be forthcoming, subject to three conditions being met. Firstly, that the tenant, Mr Stanley was in agreement, and secondly that the necessary permission was obtained from the Commissioner for Ancient Monuments. The final caveat was that anything found would belong to Mr Jones. Some months past before Nash-Williams wrote to Mr Jones's Solicitor, Mr Verity on the 11th of November citing the letter to W. Davies and detailing the proposed coming work.

My friend, Mr W.H.Davies, of Llantwit Major, has informed me of the permission kindly given by your client Mr W.T.Jones, owner of the above site, for the scientific excavation of the Roman villa, subject to the stipulations laid down in your letter 409.' MVC/AJD to Mr Davies, of 27th July, 1937.

He indicated that he hoped to begin work in the summer of 1938, subject to the necessary funds, and the relevant permissions being available. On the 16th of December 1937 Nash-Williams submitted an application for a grant in respect of the 1938 summer work to the the President of the Cambrian Archaeological Association, Mr Harold Hughes. In support of his application he emphasised the special significance of the site, pointing out that since the 1888 excavations no opportunity had arisen to continue the work, and now it was of the utmost importance that advantage should be taken without delay. '*Since the 1888 discoveries the site has, owing to local difficulties, remained closed to excavation; recently, however the property has changed hands, and the new owner has generously given his permission for the ground to be scientifically explored.*' Due to the area of the site being about an acre and a half, and in consideration that a detailed exploration would be required, he requested a grant of £300. By January 1938 Nash-Williams had written to Will Davies, who at that time was in the British School in Rome, suggesting that he would be able to excavate the site during the coming summer months. In his reply, on the 25th January, Davies offers to write to Mr Stanley, the tenant farmer whom he describes as, '*One of the straight old timers, bluff and practical and every ready to discuss local antiquities.*' In a subsequent letter, Davies proposed that he was prepared to request written permission for the excavation, from Mr Stanley and suggested a visit to Morfa Farm would be appropriate on his return from Italy in April to discuss the project with Mr Stanley and his wife.

> *I am sure they would be delighted to talk the matter over with you. If you wish, however, I will write immediately for their formal consent (which I could forward to you) and explain that I will be home by 14th April to see them personally. The proposed site of the excavation is used solely for grazing, partly for growing hay, so the question of some slight compensation would arise.*
>
> *Possibly you and I could go over and see Mr Stanley together. I think that would be much the most satisfactory plan, as your support would ensure a favourable hearing.*
>
> (W. Davies letter to Nash-Williams 31st January 1938)

Professor Davies's approach proved to be fruitful, and in a letter of 22nd of May he informed Nash-Williams that Mr Stanley had confirmed that he was quite willing for Caermead to be excavated provided the site was protected, and any damage made good. The majority of the following month proved to be occupied with a series of letters to the owners and official bodies, detailing the forthcoming investigations. Mr Verity was informed on the 13th of June of Mr Stanley's agreement for the the proposed excavations to commence. He responded the next day informing Nash-Williams that Mr Jones's architect, Mr Loveluck would be visiting the site to ensure Mr Jones interests were being considered. In order to begin his excavations, Nash-Williams, was required to seek permission from the body responsible for the custody of ancient sites, H.M. Office of Works, London. This body had been established in 1378 by the Royal household to oversee the construction of royal residences and castles. By 1815 it had passed from the Royal household to the auspices of the Treasury, and by the beginning of the First World War it included an Ancient Monuments Branch, responsible for overseeing ancient sites in Britain. On the 15th of June 1938 the H.M. Office of Works were approached for permission to excavate. This was granted, with no objections by Bryan Hugh St John O'Neil, the Assistant Inspector of Ancient Monuments, with the 20th of June being given as the commencement date. In compliance with Mr Stanley's wishes, the villa area was to be fenced before commencement of work and Nash-Williams undertook to properly fill trenches to Mr Stanley's satisfaction on completion, with an invitation to him to visit the dig as it progressed.

> *Mr Davies has told me of your wish that the field should be protected during the work and that it should be left in throughly good order afterwards. I am arranging, therefore, to have the ground carefully fenced off before digging, and I will undertake that no unauthorised persons shall be allowed on the site during the excavations and that on their all trenches will be properly filled in to your satisfaction. I trust that while the excavations are in progress you will visit them from time to time, so that I may have the opportunity of telling you of the results obtained. (Nash-Williams letter to Mr Stanley of 2nd June 1938)*

On 13th June Nash-Williams wrote to a Mr Charles Richards of Caerleon inquiring about the availability of experienced labourers to work on the dig.

I am hoping to start on a small excavation at Llantwit Major next Monday, and, as in past years, am prepared to give a start to men who have worked satisfactorily for me at Caerleon.

Conformation of labour from Mr Richards arrived by letter on the 15th, and Nash-Williams made arrangements for the use of bell tents from Charles D. Phillips of Newport, Monmouthshire, to be available from the 17th of June. Thus the bell tent, much disliked by John Storrie, made a brief appearance once more at Caermead (Figure 23). Mr Stanley was approached in the hope of providing further facilities to augment the recording of the work as it progressed *'Have you by any chance also a dry lock-up shed that I could use as a drawing office and for the storage of my instruments?'(Nash-Williams letter to Mr Stanley 13th June 1938)*. Unfortunately John Stanley did not have a shed that was available at the time, but generously offered the use of a room at Morfa House for Nash-Williams to use as an office for the duration of the work.

The excavation of the site began on the 22nd of June at the eastern barn section of the villa. This is the first entry in Nash-Williams's notebook where he records the presence of a series of banks and ditches outside the eastern wall of the barn structure. Offers to help on the dig were forthcoming from a number of student volunteers (Figure 24), that included Mr P Baker, Mr R.T.Williams, Mr H.R.Phillips and Mr Bisatt all of which had written to offer their services, together with a Mr Godfrey Davies of Balliol College,Oxford. He had written to Nash-Williams to say that had been informed of the excavations by a Miss V. Taylor, and he could offer his services as semi-skilled undergraduate labourer. Davies later provided

Nash-Williams's bell tent at Caermead. After Nash-Williams, V.E.
Archaeologia Cambrensis *102 (1953), 89-163.* (Figure 23)

Cardiff University students and others at Caermead.
Undated photograph. (Figure 24)

a number of photographs to Nash-Williams, covering areas of the excavations which Nash-Williams had not been able to acquire images of. Volunteers were offered accommodation in the tents situated on the site, or at what Nash-Williams describes as a youth hostel (possibly Woodford House) in the village, charging 25s for reasonable accommodation. In keeping with the 1888 excavations the local newspapers took an interest with the Glamorgan Gazette reporting on progress during the first week of the dig.

> *Re-excavation work commenced this week under the supervision of Mr G.V. (sic) Nash-Williams (National Museum of Wales) at Caermead, a field on Morfa Farm, Llantwit, will it is believed, prove more exciting and interesting than the finding of a Roman amphitheatre at Caerleon. Expert workmen, who have gained experience at Caerleon, are at work, and already pottery ware has been discovered. When excavation work was carried out at Caermead in 1888 (50 years ago), Mr John Storrie discovered a Roman villa. The excavation then was only partial, but the sites of several rooms were found.*
> (*Glamorgan Gazette 24th June 1938*)

> *The first newspaper to report the re-excavation work at Caermead, Llantwit Major, the Gazette will watch very carefully any further developments, such as the finding of ancient relics etc which will be fully reported. Great interest is being taken by residents of the locality, as well as far afield, for it is believed that the discoveries will, from an archaeological point of view, surpass the finding of a Roman amphitheatre at Caerleon.*
> (*Glamorgan Gazette 1st July 1938*)

The whole excavation cost £111 11s 11½d plus some outstanding items, with the bulk of the costs being for labour (Figure 25). The excavations were undertaken from the 20th June to the 30th July, and in a typed report Nash-Williams, noted that the extent of the villa was around two acres in area, with a ditch system skirting the outbuildings. He had examined the room area of the northern and western ranges and their adjunct structures, with the buildings that had been cleared, being described as in a good state of preservation. Floors were intact almost everywhere, and plaster decorated walls were found to range in height to a maximum of six feet. He completely excavated three rooms including the two partially cleared by Storrie in 1888 in which he noted that a considerable portion of the tessellated pavement remained intact. Here, in addition to the forty one skeletons discovered during the 1888 excavations four more were unearthed, encased in rough cists constructed from roofing slates (Figure 26). Nash-Williams considered that their burials were definitely Christian, probably representing a cemetery of the Early Christian Period. The Western Mail reported the skeletal finds and the local interest the excavations were producing.

A considerable amount of local interest has been aroused in the excavations and there were many visitors on Thursday.
(Western Mail and South Wales News 22nd July 1938)

Clearance of the third room in the western range, revealed well preserved remains of a furnace which had supplied a central heating system. This room showed evidence of being re-floored and used for iron smelting at a later date. Partial clearance of what was first thought to be an outbuilding of considerable size, around 80 feet by 26 feet, eventually revealed itself during later excavation to be a robustly built basilican structure. During the season many artefacts of the Roman period were unearthed, including Samian and coarse ware pottery and a number of coins. From this first excavation, the evidence accrued prompted Nash-Williams to postulate that the villa was founded in middle of 2nd century C.E and had been occupied to at least the end of the third, but that his planned further excavation work might adjust its dating.

Arrangements for the following summers work began on 8th of February 1939, with Nash-Williams writing to Mr W.T.Jones outlining a brief summary of the previous years excavations. He mentioned that the dig had aroused considerable interest in the academic community, which had resulted in the University of Wales making a grant to enable the project to continue. When the work was

Expenses of the 1938 Excavations. (Figure 25)

Photograph of the skeleton in Room 9. After Nash-Williams, V.E. Archaeologia Cambrensis 102 (1953), 89-163. (Figure 26)

complete, he stated that he intended to write a detailed report on the villa that would be published in a recognised academic journal. Once more, volunteers to help with the dig in the summer of 1939 travelled from a number of locations, including Bangor, London, Oxford and Cardiff. They included, Mr Godfrey Davies, Mr S.H.Austin Miss Eileen Clarke and Mr P.B.Baker[1]. In keeping with the previous excavation arrangements, separate accommodation for men and women volunteers was once again provided in tents. In his eventual publication on the excavations (*Archaeologia Cambrensis*, Vol. CII (1953), Part 2, pp. 89-163.), Nash-Williams acknowledges the volunteers' help, which includes a reference to the University of Utrecht in Holland, '*Able assistance with the work of digging was given by a band of willing volunteers drawn variously from the Universities of Wales, Oxford, London and Utrecht*'. Nash-Williams had an association with a Joop Fraenkel[2] who was a student at Utrecht and Chairman of the Literary Faculty of the Students Federation. Fraenkel had assisted Nash-Williams on an excavation of Sudbrook Iron Age Camp, Monmouthshire in 1934. In a letter of 15th June 1939, Fraenkel extended an invitation to Nash-Williams to deliver a series of lectures at Utrecht in the coming autumn on the topic of Roman Britain. Nash-Williams reply expressed optimism that Fraenkel would manage a return visit to Wales that summer '*I shall be excavating on my Roman villa site at Llantwit Major during the next four to five weeks, and we had both (Mrs Nash-Williams) been hoping that you might have been able to visit us for the 'dig.*' Unfortunately, Fraenkel's letter mentioned that he had been conscripted into the Dutch military, and a trip to Wales probably never occurred as by September of that year war had erupted[3].

From the entries in his field notebook the work commenced with a room at the western end of the southern range (basilican building) on Monday the 19th of June 1939. The excavations took some weeks and finished on Thursday the 13th of July 1939, the day of the last entry in the field notes, with the cost amounting to £102 02s 51½d. Although the season's excavations were complete, the site was once more proving of interest to the Cardiff Naturalists' Society, with the Western Mail reporting that the Society members had visited the site after leaving Penllyn Castle during their second field meeting of the year.

> NATURALISTS FIELD MEETING
> *Penllyn Castle, near Cowbridge the home of Col. H.R.Homfray, was one of the places visited by the Cardiff Naturalists' Society on the occasion of their second summer field meeting on Saturday. Professor William Rees spoke on the history of the castle. The party then went to Caer Mead (sic), Llantwit Major where Mr V.E. Nash-Williams gave a talk on the excavations made this year at the Roman villa.*
> (*Western Mail Monday 17th July 1939*)

In his typed report on the seasons work, having now accrued more information, Nash-Williams hypothesised that the villa originally comprised the northern and western wing, and subsequent development to the south and east resulted in a quadrangular shape. The substantial structure comprising the southern range (basilican building), he considered to be a possible residential block with a central corridor and flanking rooms. In the eastern section of this structure he described an elaborate gully system, of unknown use '*the purpose of which is at present obscure.*' Coinage uncovered here led him to consider that the building dated from the late third to early fourth century CE. To the east of the basilican building, two large barn like structures, were unearthed comprising the eastern range. These were the villa's outbuildings, utilised for farm produce and animal husbandry. On the western section of the villa complex, additional work revealed a well-preserved, channeled hypocaust linked to the furnace, unearthed in the previous year.

Coverage of the excavations by the local press, did not appear in print until the beginning of the following year, as newspapers occupied their pages with reports of conflict and military engagements. On Friday January 19th 1940, the Western Mail and South Wales News, carried an article on the excavations, reporting that they had revealed the full extent of the villa. The newspaper detailed the finds of pottery and coins, and an accompanying photograph of human remains, crudely buried in a rough coffin of roofing stones in situ across the mosaic floor, served to augment the text.

What Recent Excavations at Llantwit Major Roman Villa Revealed

New and interesting light on developments in South Wales in the Roman period has been shed by excavations recently carried out ....The villa is one of a small group of Roman villas found scattered along the South Wales sea-plain, and of interest as representing a local intrusion of the civil and agricultural life of the Roman province into the military districts of the West.

The article prompted one member of the public, a Mr Ernest George, to write to the museum with some information on what he describes as Roman regalia discovered near the villa in the mid eighteen hundreds.

Clive Arms Hotel,
360 Cowbridge Road,
Cardiff.
Jan 22/40

Dear Sir,
Reading in the Western Mail of the results of your excavations of

the old Roman Villa on the Caermead Llantwit Major, makes me think that it would be interesting for you to know that my mothers brother named David Thomas and another man were digging a trench close to the Villa, and they discovered a golden chain. The two men did not hand over the find to the authorities. Marrie Trevelyan[4] in her history of Llantwit Major asked where did the chain go to. It was taken to Cardiff and in the words of my mother sold to the Jews and put in the melting pot. They secured one hundred pounds. I was given to understand that my uncle bought a horse and cart with his fifty pounds. After all there was not much encouragement in handing over treasure trove in those days. My mother told me that she saw the chain and that the links were about two inches long. I have no doubt that it was a part of Roman Regalia. This happened about the year 1856. I was twice within a couple of hundred yards of the Villa. Your illustrations of the central heating is very similar to those I saw at Gelligaer when they opened the Roman Fort in 1900 and a few years later which probably you saw.

I was very disappointed at the meagre results of the excavating of the old college of learning in Llantwit Major a couple of years ago a wonderful old town.
Yours sincerely,
Ernest E.George.

On an 1885 Ordinance Survey map of the Caermead area, there is a cross symbol stating Gold Torque (sic) found here AD 1861 (Figure 27). The Torque or Torc was uncovered by two workmen digging a drain at Lachas Moor, located few hundred yards to the east of the villa in the ownership of a Mr C.Wilkins, the brother of Mrs Ellen Murley's father, Evan. The 1840 tithe map identifies the land as parcel 267, moorland, owned by the Reverend Robert Nicholl and occupied by Christopher Wilkins at a tithe cost of £0 1s 6d. The discovery of a gold chain or Torc was reported in the Western Mail of 6th January 1886 and the same report appeared in *Archaeologia Cambrensis* (1887) Vol. IV, p. 155 where it was described:

> *as heavy as a pound of butter and nearly as soft, a sign of the purity of the gold. We have, however, not been able to ascertain the pattern, or in whose possession it now is; but Mr C. Wilkins, the owner of the land, put in a claim for it.*

Nash-Williams considered both Mr George's letter and the Archaeologia article were referring to the same object, namely a piece of Roman regalia. In a collection of papers at Llantwit Major Local History Society Archive belonging to the late Professor William Davies, one details the discovery of the gold Torc. This letter is possibly attributed to his uncle Frank and provides the following information:

> *Account of Discovery in the Lachas Moors, Llantwit Major.*
> *The golden torque or "chain" as it is locally called, was found by Hopkin Hopkin, and David Thomas between the "little Wetmoor field" and the Laclias (sic) Moors beside the Caermead.* ~~Hopkin and Thomas were sinking a drain on that spot~~ (crossed out text). *Hopkin now is my informant says the "chain" as he calls it resembled a thick cord as of gold. It consisted of 6 pieces connected by flat "bars" placed apart at equal distances. In the centre of the "chain" these are as "one plain piece" exactly like the pendulum of an old clock. Each end of the "chain" was "finished off with a loop".* ~~Hopkin~~ (crossed out text)*the old man says he thought the "chain" was part of "a Kings equipmentals" (sic)* ~~buried~~ (crossed out text) *concealed by the bearer in the earth at a time of danger and forgotten by the owners.*
>
> ~~*It had the appearance of having been thrust in the earth*~~*.* (crossed out text)
> *It was found about 2 feet 9 inches in the earth and covered with stuff which he (sic) Hopkin calls the "mother of coal"*

> *Weight 1 lb (sic) 1 lb sold in Cardiff reserve £3-10 ? ounce Also details of sale*
>
> ~~*About the same time*~~ (crossed out text) *Soon afterwards Thomas Lewis found a gold spoon in the same neighbourhood. W. Price (then of Flanders) of Bridgend saw him just as he found it, and gave him 1/6 (sic)2/6 for the spoon.*
>
> *Lewis became frightened because he frequently saw a fine and stately man with a three cornered hat who appeared about "milking time"* ~~*in the spring & summer.*~~ (crossed out text)

The letter contains a small drawing of the Torc (Figure 28). Because pre-Roman occupants of Britain also wore torcs, its origins cannot be assigned to the Roman period, with any confidence, and without the article itself, no definitive date for its manufacture can be determined. Its connection to the Iron Age site, preceding the villa at Caermead, or the Roman occupation there remains speculative, but distinctly possible, given the location of its discovery.

In 1940 Nash-Williams was enlisted in the army as a Major in the Historical Section of the War Office, remaining in service until 1945, and in consequence the planned final seasons work of that year was postponed. It was during his military service, that the Western Mail reported that he was to be awarded the degree of Doctor of Litteris by the University of Wales for his studies of Roman Wales.

> *Mr Victor Erle Nash-Williams, keeper of Archaeology at the National Museum of Wales, Cardiff, son of Mr R.Nash-Williams and Mrs. Williams has been awarded the degree of Doctor of Litteris by the Academic Board of the University of Wales.*
> *(Western Mail, Friday 26th July 1940)*

In the spring of 1948 the project was resurrected, once again under the auspices of the National Museum of Wales and

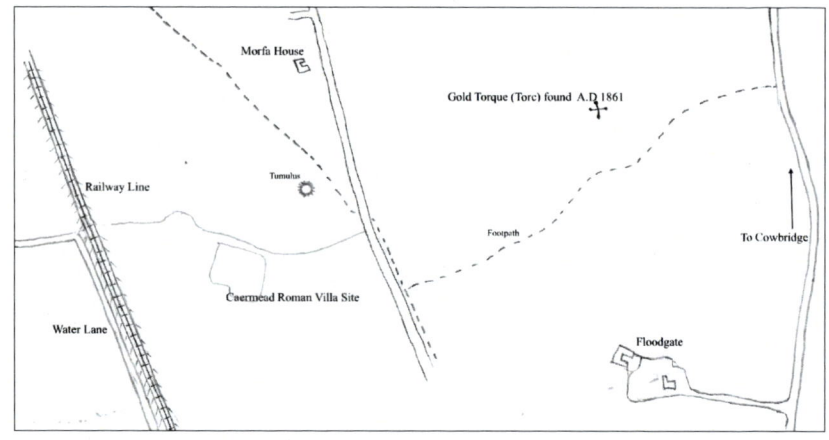

Map of Caermead area showing location of gold torque find in 1861.
(Figure 27)

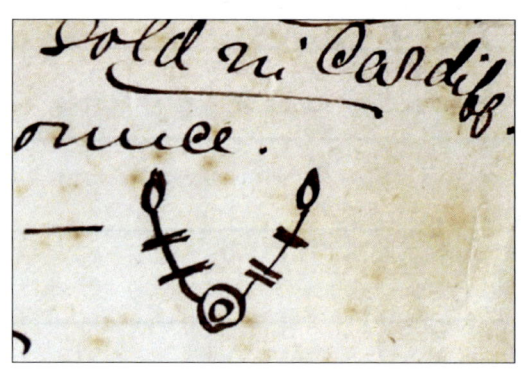

Drawing of the Gold Torc from Professor W.Davies letter. (Figure 28)

directorship of Dr Nash-Williams. As the Keeper of Archaeology he wrote to the Director of the Museum on the 17th of April 1948, seeking approval for a final season's work, indicating that subject to certain stipulations by the owner and tenant, the site was once more available for excavation for a limited time. The work was to be undertaken from the 28th of June to 31st of July and would finally allow him to publish his findings.

> *So that I can complete publication of the villa, in common with other outstanding reports which have been delayed by circumstances outside my control. Difficulties of finance, labour,*

etc, render it unlikely that I shall be able to make the proposed work fully definitive, but I hope at least to "round off" the excavation to the point of possible publication.

The undertaking of course depends on my being able to raise the necessary excavation funds, and in this I may be successful.

Post war austerity dictated an approach to multiple organisations in order to secure sufficient funding needed for the project, and to facilitate this Nash-Williams began writing to a number of bodies to request grants. On the 13th of May he submitted an application for a grant to Thomas Jones Pierce the Secretary of the Cambrian Archaeology Association at The University College of Wales, Aberystwyth, noting that he was anxious to complete the project but that the cost would be treble that of the previous work at an estimated £350.0. The Treasurer of the Association, Mr H J.Randall, replied on the 31st of May to confirm that although some members of the committee made observations on the high cost, they resolved to make a grant of £150.0, subject to a full report on the whole excavations being published in a reasonable time. The monies were provided from the Association's Research Funds and sent to Nash-Williams on the 8th of June. Further funding of £130 was obtained from the University of Wales, Board of Celtic Studies, in addition to monies from The National Museum of Wales and a token grant from the Cardiff Naturalists' Society. The funds received were deposited in Nash-Williams (Number 3) account at Lloyds Bank, Fleur-De-Lys, Bargoed, a town to which he had childhood links. He was born there in August 21st 1897 and on the 1911 census can be found residing with his grandmother, Mary Nash, whilst attending Lewis School, Pengam.

The month of May proved to be a particularly busy time, with letters to equipment suppliers W Clarke of 98, Cardiff

Road requesting fencing, planks and wheelbarrows and to Charles D. Phillips of Newport in respect of tents. Approaches were made to the Department of Archaeology (Cardiff University) for a limited number of students to participate with an offer of accommodation provided in on-site tents. Experienced workers who took part in the previous excavations were once again sought through Mr Charles Richards of 12 Lodge Avenue, Caerleon. In a letter dated 26th of May Mr Richards indicated that all were now in full employment and he (Richards), was unable to undertake strenuous digging due to medical advice with respect to a serious injury sustained during the war, but could assist with light duties. Nash-Williams subsequently offered him a post of general handyman/watchman at 10s per day with the possibility of an extra pound or two at the end of the dig. Once again Nash-Williams requested the help of Professor W. H. Davies in a letter of the 20th of May to try and resolve concerns of a local nature. Davies replied on the 31st outlining his progress liaising with the employment exchange for workers, and sourcing fencing from the local ironmonger in an effort to solve the difficulties arising with materials and labour availability. Post war, fencing was difficult to obtain without the necessary permits but Davies mentioned that Mr H. Andrews might be able to circumvent paperwork to obtain some. He also recommended a formal approach to the Glamorgan Agricultural Committee for assistance. It is clear from his correspondence, that Nash-Williams was hoping to begin on 21st of June but had concerns regarding his own accommodation in Llantwit Major for the duration of the excavations. In respect of this, Davies referred to a conversation with a Mrs. T. Price of Kenilworth, whose dwelling he thought would be the most convenient place. He confirmed that Mrs Price was prepared to consider simple meals, but Davies noted she might change her mind as his letter expressed the salient point of post war food shortages with the poignant phrase *'food is everybody's bugbear these days.'* On the 4th of June Nash-Williams wrote to Mrs Price, mentioning that his friend Professor Davies had suggested her premises as suitable accommodation for the duration of the excavations. Conscious of the post war food situation he approached this subject diplomatically, emphasising that he only required simple meals.

With regard to meals, I am a very simple person, and the plainer my meals are, the better they suit me. As I should be out all day, the best arrangement for me would be a plain break-fast, sandwiches for lunch, a high tea (bully beef or a boiled egg, etc.), and a light supper of bread and butter and tea. I do not want cooked meals. My only need is a sitting-room where I could work quietly in the evenings.

Mrs Price, in reply confirmed that accommodation would be secured from the 28th June to the end of July at a cost of £4 per week and that Nash-Williams was to bring his house slippers! By the 14th of June, as things gradually fell into place, Nash-Williams wrote to the tenant of Morfa Farm, Mr John Stanley saying that although he was encountering difficulties, he was looking forward to beginning excavations on the 28th of June.

I am encountering difficulties at every turn in trying to arrange the work, but I hope to surmount them all. I am negotiating for some fencing to fence off the site, and shall if possible arrange for the wire and the men to arrive on or about the 25th June, so that the fencing may be put up ready for digging to start in earnest on 28th June.

In regard to fencing the site, Professor Davies had made a visit to Caermead and paced the area to produce a rough plan, annotated with dimensions and indicating the position of a

Professor W. Davies's fencing plan. (Figure 29)

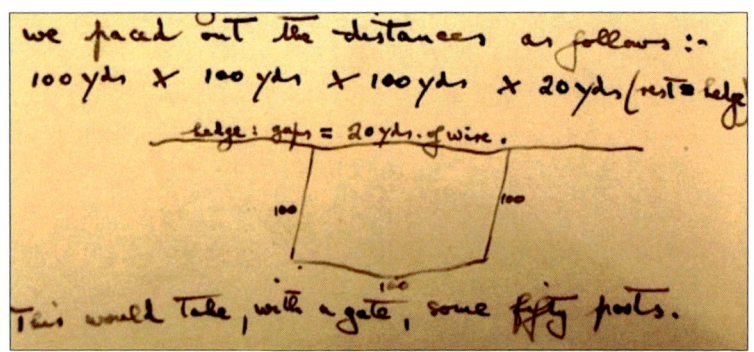

Ministry of Road Haulage paperwork detaining supply and return of fencing material. (Figure 30)

possible gate access (Figure 29). He had also made arrangements with Mr Hughie Andrews, the local Postmaster, to be at the site to supervise the erection of the wire fencing, on arrival of materials from the Ministry of Works Road Haulage (Figure 30). Labourers[5] were also required to remove the top layers of soil before the student volunteers could assist Nash-Williams in the archaeological excavations, and to effect this he had written to the local Employment Exchange to source suitable workers. The manager of the Exchange was Mr Alfie Davies, well known to Hughie Andrews and William Davies. He provided a number of men, who Nash-Williams considered had solved a difficult problem for him, *'such people were essential for the excavations success as my plans is to open up the site as rapidly and extensively as possible.'* His field notes confirm that he commenced work on the 25th June of 1948. The Glamorgan Gazette of Friday the 2nd of July reported on the excavations, and the following Friday edition of the 9th of July it published an article detailing the finds. As with the previous excavations, other local newspapers followed the progress and informed readers of the quality and size of the remains.

Llantwit Major Roman Excavations

Important light has been shed on developments in South Wales in the Roman period by excavations now in progress on the site of a Roman villa at Llantwit Major, under the direction of Dr V.E. Nash-Williams, of the National Museum of Wales, Cardiff and Cardiff University College.

The results to date show that the villa was a large, well-ordered, and substantially built establishment, comparable in size and plan with some of the larger villas found in the Cotswold region.

(Western Mail and South Wales News Monday 26th July 1948)

The excavations were completed on the 30th of July 1948, and in contrast to the 1888 work, a more extensive clearance of the site had been undertaken over the 1938 to 1948 period[6] (Figure 31). Nash-Williams cleared a number of the rooms and dug trenches (marked alphabetically; Figure 32) along specific sections of the remains. His work revealed a substantial series of buildings, surrounding a large courtyard bordered on the eastern approach by a considerable length of banks and ditches. The ditch/bank system is referred to in the first entry in his field notebook dated the 22nd of July 1938. It began just to the south of the hedge at the northern end of Caermead field and extended for some 475 feet in a southernly direction. The bank averaged 15 feet in width and varied from a few inches to 2.5 feet in height. Overall, the ditches were V shaped being 10 feet in width at the top, 4 feet in depth and and narrowing to around 4 feet width at the base (Figure 31). Cuttings (K-l, M-N and O-P Figure 31,32,33) were made across the system, and the results led to the general conclusion that it could have been constructed contemporaneously with the villa and may have been capped with hedgerows or timber fencing. The purpose of which was considered to be simply that of restriction of stock entering the villa itself or as a measure of privacy. Nash-Williams speculated that the ditch and bank system could have enclosed the villa on all four sides, with the ditch providing useful drainage for a generally moist site. The ditch/bank system was dated to around the middle of the second century (circa 150 CE) determined by odd sherds of pottery found in the occupation layer. The north-east run of the bank was interrupted at a point exterior to Building C (Figure 33) by a gap of around 15 feet, which may have been a gate-opening, allowing passage to the villa's working areas. Once through the gap in the bank, access to the villa's large eastern yard was through an approximately 10 feet wide gateway and passage between Buildings C and A. From here, the bank continued in a south-easterly direction before terminating abruptly in an open field. At the northern section of the complex, access was provided to the working area by an approximately 18 feet gap between Building A and the workshop complex. To the south, access to the villa courtyard and adjoining domiciliary structures of the western and northerly range was provided by a gap in the wall section of around 14 feet.

The villa itself was roughly quadrangular in shape,

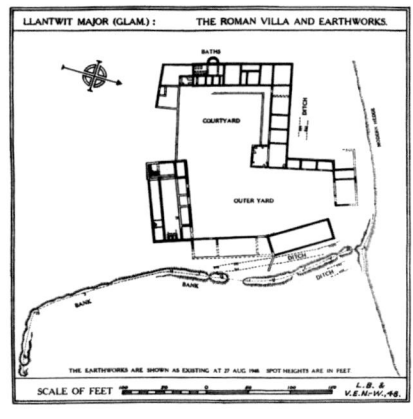

Plan of villa and earthworks. After Nash-Williams, V.E. Archaeologia Cambrensis 102 (1953), 89-163. (Figure 31)

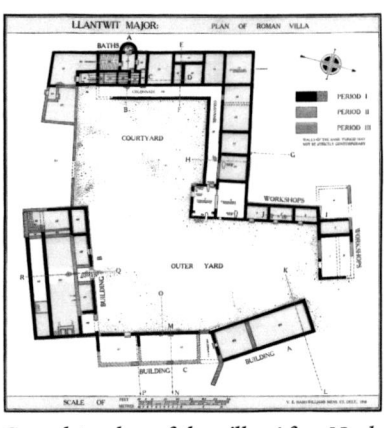

Complete plan of the villa. After Nash-Williams, V.E. Archaeologia Cambrensis 102 (1953), 89-163.33. (Figure 33)

consisting of four main sections enclosing a spacious central open area (Figure 33). This comprised a large yard on the eastern side conjoined to an inner courtyard at the west. The whole villa complex measured approximately 240 feet east to west by 256 feet north to south being some one-and-a-half acres in area. The western and adjacent northern wings were composed of domestic buildings which linked to workshops at the easternmost end. A range of workshop and barn structures

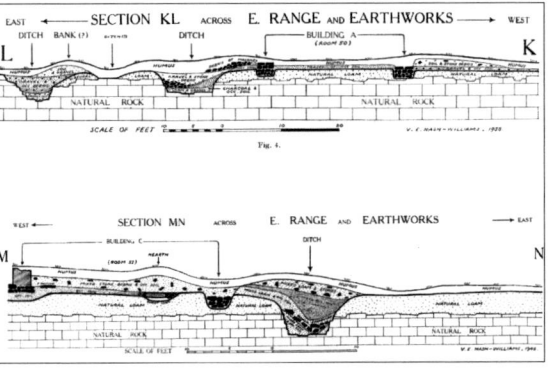

Example of sections across the earthworks (banks and ditches). After Nash-Williams, V.E. Archaeologia Cambrensis 102 (1953), 89-163.33. (Figure 32)

enclosed the outer yard on the north and eastern ranges, whilst the southern range was composed of a large basilican-type structure. The main materials used in the construction were local limestone and sandstone, with the masonry of the walls consisting of rubble, coursed roughly and bound by a matrix of hard, white limy mortar. This mortar was also used as an external render to the buildings. A subsequent report on the stone by Nash-Williams's colleague, Dr F.J.North concluded that it closely resembled the Rhaetic sandstone exposed around the St. Hilary area and that could be regarded as its source. A number of quernstones and fragments discovered were of Rhaetic sandstone, resembling the type at nearby Stormy Down or the Coity/Coychurch area. The limestone and sandstone blocks were supplemented where necessary, by columns, finials and ridges etc of Bath Stone, akin to Oolite quarried from the Bath region of Somerset. The Bath Stone may have made the journey to the villa, by boat across the Bristol Channel, which would have been a much easier route in terms of time and effort, compared to the alternative, long overland route around the channel coast. A convenient and possible landing site could have been at an ancient port, sited at the entrance to or in the Colhugh valley, as suggested by Professor William Davies in his typed notes, Llantwit and its Past.

> *The remains of an early harbour, though the topography is entirely changed, are still visible: the piles of the breakwater, some eighty in number, are known to-day by the name of the "Black Men" while the foundation of a stone wharf can be traced some distance to their left (east). Nearby coins of Claudius, Nero and Vaspasian are said to have been found. The port was in use as late as the sixteenth century.*

In 1966, a sample of wood was taken from the "Black Boys, as they are known today, by Professor Davies and submitted to an

American Company, Isotopes, of New Jersey via the University of Wales, Aberystwyth to undergo radiocarbon dating. This analysis returned a date of circa 1400. Recent (2019) oxygen isotope dendrochronology undertaken by Swansea University and The University of Wales Trinity St Davids has returned a date of spring 1435 for the oak used. Both these figures are indicative of the date that the oak was felled but confirm that the structure is medieval and not Roman in origin. The stone wharf referred to by Professor Davies to the east of the Black Boys is still visible and in June 2009, the access ramp at the beach was cleared of boulders by the local authority, revealing a causeway of large flat stones extending around 30 feet seaward. No archaeological examination was performed at the time, and therefore no date can be assigned to the causeway, but it remains an intriguing find. Although there is no direct evidence indicating the presence of a small Roman port or landing, its existence cannot be discounted, as both the beach area and the Colhugh River flowing seaward through the Colhugh Valley would be accessible by flat bottomed boats. A rudimentary dock sited here would utilise the Bristol Channel waterway, allowing a quicker and easier movement of bulky goods from the Somerset coast to South Wales, rather than via a protracted road journey around the Seven Estuary. The supposition that the Bristol Channel appears to have been utilised as a transport avenue is given support by discoveries of fragments of a late third-century vessel, uncovered at Magor, and slate from the Prescelly Mountains in Pembrokeshire found at the Roman wharves at Caerleon. It has also been suggested that the forts at Cardiff and Neath, although military sites, probably also acted as harbours for a Seven Estuary Fleet. Large legionary fortresses, were regularly sited on navigable rivers or estuaries as in the case of Caerleon, Chester and York because in the Roman world it was cheaper and easier to transport goods by water than overland. The unexpected discovery of coal at the villa (see later) is considered by Professor William Manning in his book *A Pocket Guide Roman Wales*, to be indicative of supplies being transported to consumers in the Vale of Glamorgan by coastal vessels. Although no evidence remains of a definitive route from the beach to the villa, a consideration of the topography would suggest transport along the Colhugh Valley, continuing upwards on a path of convenient slope to Caermead.

From the lack of heavy nails and larger size bolts present at the villa site, it was conjectured that the walls of the villa were of solid construction to roof height and not capped by an wooden upper layer. The profusion of lighter nails (some still in the roofing slabs), led to the conclusion that the roof consisted of the traditional Roman timber construction using nailed joints. In the British climate, the roof would have had a pitch between twenty to thirty degrees to allow efficient water run-off, without losing tiles due to an overly steep slope. The original roof of the domestic part of the villa may have been red clay tile (*tegulae and imbrice*), as examples were discovered on site, but it was probably replaced in due course by hexagonal and pentagonal slabs of flaggy Pennant sandstone. These slabs were also used on most of the roofs of the associated buildings in the complex and attached to the wooded roof framework by a nail driven through a hole situated at one end. Sandstone of this nature occurs locally between Aberkenfig and Llanilid, and would have provided a convenient local source material. The roof finial excavated by Storrie was Bath stone akin to Oolite of the Coombe Down stone which together with the Bath limestone ridge pieces, provided a high standard of finish to the roofing (Figure 34).

Inference of there being an upper storey over the domiciliary region of the villa is suggested by the size and position of the walls of Rooms 17 and 18 which may have acted as a stairwell. This conjecture is reinforced by the notably solid construction of the party walls in this region and the layout of the walls which are passage like in arrangement. If an upper clerestory existed it could have either been used for storage or acted as a separate storey. Pieces of window-glass uncovered on the site indicated the presence of glazed windows to the main villa building and the bath suite. The glass was either colourless or had a bluish or greenish tint, varying in thickness from two to three millimetres. One side of the glass was smooth and clear whilst the other was rough and opaque. The interior walls of the domestic range were rendered with a fine painted wall-plaster, which was adorned with three decorative styles. A panelled decoration comprised a white field-edge with border lines of various colours such as yellow, green, orange, red, crimson, light-blue, mauve and black, whilst a floral design consisted of leaves and scrolls in red and green on a white background. Other fragments of plaster surface were decorated with a marbled pattern comprising a background of pale-blue or pale-mauve with splashes of cream, buff, red, crimson, purple and dark-blue. This style is similar to the "Incrustation" style used at Pompeii.

The floors of most of the living spaces in the domiciliary section were of *opus signinum*, Opus derives from a "work or construction", and signinum, "after the fashion of Signa", a small town near Rome; essentially it is a mortar mix with added crushed brick or terracotta. This was also present on a number of the room walls, especially the bath block. In Rooms 8 and 9 (Figure 35) at the end of the north range Storrie had uncovered the decorated mosaic pavement, and these two rooms, from their size and ornateness, were identified as the principal reception rooms. Room 9, 22 feet 6 inches by 16 feet 6 inches, had a small vestibule at the eastern end (9a) which possibly

Conjectural reconstruction of part of the roof. After Nash-Williams, V.E. Archaeologia Cambrensis 102 (1953), 89-163.33. (Figure 34)

Rooms 8 and 9. After Nash-Williams, V.E. Archaeologia Cambrensis 102 (1953), 89-163.33. (Figure 35)

opened onto the courtyard via a door. Once inside the vestibule, entrance to the main area of Room 9 was through a wide opening in its western wall (possibly, originally screened with a curtain) which mirrored the intercommunication between Room 9 and Room 8, (26 feet 6 inches by 20 feet). In

Room 8 the walls had been faced with two coats of plaster, the earlier coat painted with multi-coloured horizontal bands of varying sizes in colours such as white, blue, yellow ochre, crimson and red. Covering this earlier coat was an upper, later layer imitating marble with a base colour of pale-blue, speckled with flecks of dark-blue and crimson.

The mosaics in Room 9/9a presented as a surround of plain brown tesserae enclosing a narrow border of four-cord interlacing pattern in red, white and blue, which framed a pattern of blue frets on a white background. In Room 8, a similar surround existed which enclosed a complex pattern of symmetrically arranged squares and roundels filled with plaitwork and rosette motifs, interspersed with smaller lozenges and triangles of chequer work. The whole pattern was worked in red, blue, white and two shades of green and had an almost "Celtic" appearance (Figure 36). In both these rooms Storrie had uncovered a number of human skeletons, and the Nash-Williams excavation unearthed some thirteen in Rooms 9/9a and twenty eight in Room 8, together with the remains of two horses. The skeletons comprised twenty five male, one female and two children, found in a variety of positions except four that had been a distinct burial. A number of complete skeletons were revealed, some in rough stone cists which transversed the room walls, and others over-buried with subsequent bodies and orientated east to west. It was considered that they were not attributable to a massacre as suggested by Storrie, but formal Christian internment, after the villa had become a ruin, as in three cases their cists were cut through the walls of the villa room.

Westerly from Rooms 9/9a were found a series of further rooms 10 to 14 which were thought to have comprised the main living apartments of the villa, including the dining room or *triclinium*, kitchen and service rooms. Room 10, 20 feet wide by

The mosaic floor in Room 8. After Nash-Williams, V.E. Archaeologia Cambrensis *102 (1953), 89-163.33.* (Figure 36)

Room 14 looking east 1888. From Storrie's original notebook. (Figure 37)

15 feet long, showed evidence of a concrete floor and walls rendered with plaster panelled in white, red, crimson and dark ochre. Removal of the debris and soil covering the floor, revealed a skeleton of an adult female, which Nash-Williams considered to have been buried in a long since decayed wooden

coffin when the villa was a ruin. Rooms 11 to 14 were 20 feet in width and varied in length at 15 feet 6 inches, 19 feet, 13 feet, and 23 feet. with Room 14 being the most interesting. It was proposed that this room might have served as a sitting or dressing room during cold weather, as clearance by Storrie revealed a hypocaust with an exterior furnace providing a flow of hot air via an arched flue in the north wall. The hypocaust was constructed of stone channels arranged in an irregular herring-bone pattern, (Figure 37) supporting a floor of tiles, which were pierced by holes of between one and a quarter to two and a half inches in diameter. Possibly, a charcoal fuelled furnace would have provided the hot air that passed directly from the hypocaust through the small vents in each floor tile to warm the room. The remaining rooms may well have been heated by use of portable braziers, as was common practice elsewhere in the colder northern European regions of the empire. The room sequence of the northern range continued along the western range with possible bedrooms, and upper level, forming a section between the principal living rooms to the north side and the bath suite to the west.

An 8 feet wide colonnaded paved veranda, Room 15 and 20, ran along the front of the domestic range and continued to the end of the bathhouse section, providing access to the rooms. The outer wall of the veranda, was of a flimsy construction, bedded directly onto the soil with no foundations and probably acted as a sleeper-wall or plinth carrying a row of columns to support its roof. A fragmented column drum (Figure 38) of 8 inches diameter was found outside Room 12 which had a hollow or socket carved out on one side which might have provided anchorage for a wooden rail. In warmer climates such a colonnade would have been open, but in Britain, due to the cold and wind, the lower section may have been enclosed, perhaps with a wooden partition to provide shelter.

The colonnade may well have possessed its own dwarf roof or been sited under an extended overhang from the main roof. Where the colonnade met the principal villa room (Room 9) Storrie, recorded the discovery of two column drums. A possible use of these was proposed by Professor J.M.C.Toynbee in the 1970s who suggested that a statue of Fortuna and another statue, a fragment which was discovered by Nash-Williams, may have flanked the entrance to Room 9, standing in niches (a conjecture from the statue of Fortuna which had a non-representational back). This would have created an imposing entrance into the principal reception room (Room 9) for visitors, and also projected an aura of wealth and importance of the owners. Clearance of the colonnade revealed the skeleton of another female, oriented east to west, with a damaged skull, which looked as if it had been crushed by the weight of material above it. At its left shoulder was a coin of the Emperor Carausius (CE 286-93) which Nash-Williams considered to be associated with the skeleton. At the north-west angle of the wall of the colonnade, two coats of well preserved plaster remained. The earlier one was red faced with a later coat imitating a marble finish comprising of pale-blue flecked with dark-blue and red. The remainder of the veranda contained only the earlier coat of plaster, and flanked Rooms 16 to 21, which may have opened directly into it through doorways in their walls. These rooms may have had a dual function, primarily as the sleeping quarters, but also doubling up as disrobing rooms for users of the adjoining bath suite. As in the northerly range the floors were of *opus signinum* and plaster rendered walls. An unexplained feature of Room 21 was a narrow ledge of *opus signinum* 2 feet 9 inches wide against the western wall, which may have been the remains of a border of an original timber floor, which had eventually perished.

The Bath Suite

The bath suite was a substantial structure comprising a compact, self-contained, ten room arrangement (Figure 39). The baths were solidly built with the majority of walls bedded directly onto natural rock. The suite comprised a full sequence of cold and hot rooms, with floors of smooth pink concrete (*opus signinum*) and walls generally rendered in plaster, except those of the cold and hot plunge (Rooms 27 and 30) areas which were coloured *opus signinum*. The cold bath and also the *frigidarium* may have been vaulted with tufa blocks, a porous limestone utilised to insulate a vault. In his report, Dr. J. North considered a possible source of the tufa to be from deposits associated with a hard-water spring located in the Vale of Glamorgan possibly near Llancarfan.

Entrance to the bath suite was gained from the veranda via Room 22 (10 feet 6 inches long and 3 feet wide) which originally had walls of plaster, coloured with white and crimson bands, but was later redecorated with pale-blue flecked with splashes of dark blue and crimson in a marble imitation. At its end there may have been a door leading into the smaller Room 23, (7 feet by 12 feet), which probably served as an undressing room (*apodyterium*) decorated with the same plaster coat as Room 22. Room 24, 10 feet 6 inches long and 10 feet wide was the cold room (*frigidarium*) and the first of the bath rooms proper, and probably had been finished originally with a cold basin to enable the bather to douche themselves with cool water at the start and end of the bathing process. Here the bather would also anoint themselves with unguents in preparation for skin scraping to remove dirt. The walls had been rendered with *opus signinum*, covered with a smooth plaster coat that was adorned with white panels, edged in crimson on which were painted floral designs in green, pink and purple. In the detritus on the *opus signinum* floor, the excavation revealed scraps of clear

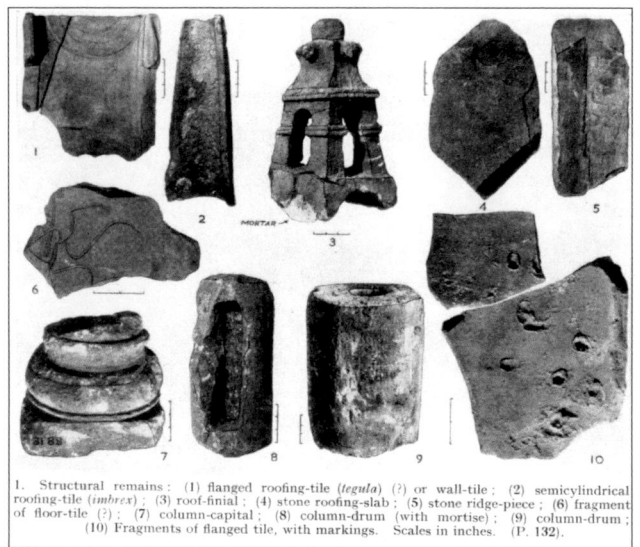

Structural remains including the column drum. After Nash-Williams, V.E. Archaeologia Cambrensis 102 (1953), 89-163.33. (Figure 38)

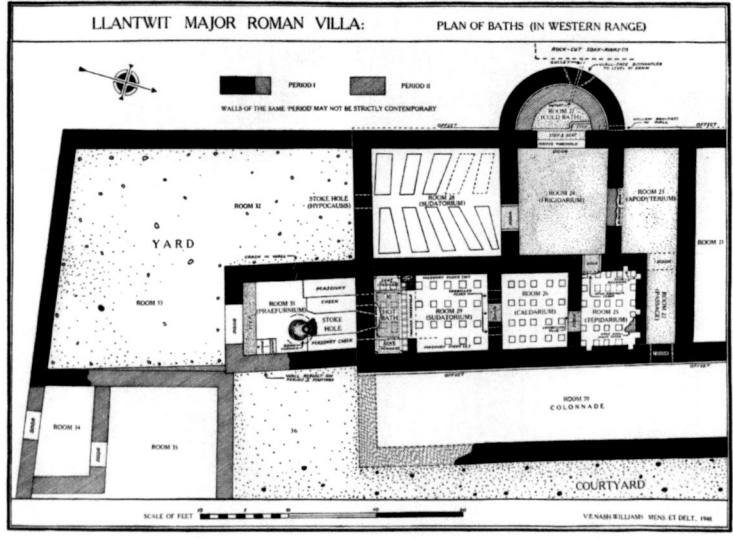

Plan of the bath suite. After Nash-Williams, V.E. Archaeologia Cambrensis 102 (1953), 89-163.33. (Figure 39)

window glass, and also remains of cut tufa which had probably been used to construct a barrel shape or vaulted roof.

Adjacent to this room, forming an alcove to the *frigidarium* was the cold bath or *piscina* Room 27, 10 feet in internal diameter, containing a sunk floor of *opus signinum*, and used by the bather to cool after passing through the heated areas (Figure 40). The initial entrance was decorated in light pink which had at some point been covered with a darker layer of pink-red colouration. The *piscina* had a colour wash of deep crimson over the wall space, floor and inside of the bath. Drainage of the bath was through a floor-level plughole set in the apse wall leading to a lead outlet pipe, which discharged its contents into a soak away, cut into the rock, external to the wall (Figure 41). A hollow box-tile which passed transversely through the wall, some two feet above the bath bottom, may have been used as a water inlet through a pipe from an external water supply. The nearby spring, Ffynnon Caer-medd would be a likely source. Although there is no evidence of any water transport system from the spring directly to the bath suite, it remains a distinct possibility in consideration of the quality of the villa's construction. The accumulated detritus clearance here unearthed tufa voussoirs (a wedge shaped or tapered stone used to construct an arch), suggesting that the bath roof had originally been vaulted with a half dome.

The hot bath area, Rooms 25 (*Tepidarium* [warm room]), 26 (*Caldarium* [hot room]), 28 (*Sudatorium* [sweating chamber]) and 29 (*Sudatorium*) of the suite were heated by means of a hypocaust system (Figure 42). This was constructed of the usual brick pilae of 8 inch square tiles extending to around 3 feet in height supporting the floor above. The action of hot air flowing around the pilae over a protracted period had eroded the tile edges to a rounder shape, giving them a slightly circular appearance. Heat from the furnace (*praefurnium*, Room

31) was transferred largely by convection to the hypocaust system under Rooms 29, 26 and 25, through flues lined with tegulae. These were 12 to 15 inches wide and 2 feet high situated in the south wall of the bath suite and capable of delivering a constant and considerable flow of hot air from the furnace. Heat was also transferred in a vertical direction, by air flow through box-tile flues recessed into the walls of the hot rooms before discharging through small clay cowls at roof height. The combination of both these methods delivered an efficient heating system to the bath rooms and effected a thermal gradient from maximum at Room 28 (*Sudatorium*) to a minimum at Room 25 (*Tepidarium*). Thus the bather could move in comfort, from a warm to a hot environment, gradually accustoming themselves to the increase in ambient temperature. The floors of the rooms above the hypocaust would eventually become very hot, especially those situated nearest the furnace, and to protect their feet, bathers would have had to wear foot protection.

Room 25 the *Tepidarium* was some 6 feet by 9 feet in size and was entered through a narrow doorway from Room 24. The walls were painted red and mauve flecked with purple and buff, with a floor of pink *opus signinum*. This room led to the hotter *Caldarium*, Room 26, (8 feet 6 inches by 9 feet) through a doorway in the north wall, and onto the *Sudatorium* Room 29, which had walls decorated in a panelled pattern, in white, crimson, pink purple and black. Clearance here revealed traces of plaster with a marble pattern of pale-mauve and purple and also pieces of floor material, coloured in panels of white and crimson. Room 30, (3 feet 10 inches by 9 feet) contained the hot bath (*alveus*) and was connected to Room 29 by an arched opening carried on side piers. The walls and a floor were of pinkish-white *opus signinum*. Below the floor was a 3 feet deep hypocaust constructed of the usual 8 inch square tile pilae,

Photographs of the cold bath. After Nash-Williams, V.E. Archaeologia Cambrensis 102 (1953), 89-163.33. (Figure 40)

Photograph of the cold bath outflow. After Nash-Williams, V.E. Archaeologia Cambrensis 102 (1953), 89-163.33. (Figure 41)

Photograph of the hypocaust system showing the brick pili. After Nash-Williams, V.E. Archaeologia Cambrensis 102 (1953), 89-163.33. (Figure 42)

which again had been worn to a circular shape by the hot airflow. The presence of box tiles suggested that heat from the hypocaust may have been channelled into the room to augment the heating of the bath, which would have been filled with hot water produced in the furnace room (Room 31, see below).

The transport of hot water into the bath may well have been a manual task as no inlet pipe was apparent during the clearance. Room 28 (Figure 43) another *Sudatorium* or *laconicum* was a spacious chamber 15 feet in length by 12 feet 6 inches in width with access gained from the *frigidarium*, Room 24. This chamber had its own source of heat via a stoke-hole discharging under the floor through a flue in the south wall. In this room, however the hypocaust system was of a different construction from the other bathrooms as it consisted of large rectangular stone blocks which acted as substantial pilae. These blocks were around 3 feet in depth and consisted of large rock fragments, coated in mortar arranged in a herringbone pattern. In the south wall of this room an arched stoke-hole 1 foot 6 inches wide and 2 feet 6 inches high, composed of tiles and stonework provided heat to the hypocaust. The absence of soot here suggested that unlike the main bath rooms this furnace utilised charcoal and not wood as a fuel, thus producing a smokeless heat that could have been directly admitted to the room above. Once again, the discovery of glass fragments alluded to the possibility of there being windows present.

Overall, the whole bath complex was finished to a high standard and must have looked quite impressive, adorned with coloured walls and floors in, pastel colours, creating a relaxing atmosphere for the bather. The warm room (25) at the end of the heating system would have been the starting point of the sweating process for the bather, whilst in the hot Room (26), copious perspiration was induced by maintaining a high ambient temperature. To complete the process, Room 29, the hottest area, was used by the bather to cleanse the skin by vigorously scraping it with the strigil before using the adjoining hot bath (*alveus*). In contrast to the moist heat experienced in these rooms, Room 28 the second sweating chamber was designed to deliver dry heat, which according to Roman practice would have been the most comfortable way to complete the bathing process before returning to the open air. Roman bath suites were generally lit by narrow lancet windows glazed with pale green glass and remains of glass unearthed in the courtyard were either clear, bluish tinted or faintly green with one rough and one smooth face, varying in thickness from two to three millimeters. Conceivably this type of glass was used in both the bath and domestic room windows.

The furnace (*praefurnium*), Room 31, 13 feet long by 7 feet 6 inches wide, provided the heat to the hypocaust of the bathrooms by means of a large arched flue (Figure 44) 2 feet 6 inches wide by 3 feet high composed of large sandstone voussoirs, cemented together with a bright red tile dust mortar. The furnace itself produced heat from a fire pit (*hypocausis*) sited on the south wall of Room 30. Flanking the fire pit were two masonry cheeks, approximately 2 feet 6 inches in height, which served as a support for metal cistern(s) (*vasa*) used to heat water for the hot bath in the adjoining room (Room 30). The furnace chamber showed signs of structural stress due to the cyclical heating and cooling over a protracted period, which had resulted in a crack in the west wall. The consequence of this was that the southern half had shrunk and settled causing a collapse of the eastern half, which had been roughly rebuilt at some time.

To run the hypocaust system a considerable amount of fuel would have been required to supply the two furnaces. This was probably wood or charcoal, and may have been stored in the

Room 28. After Nash-Williams, V.E. Archaeologia Cambrensis *102 (1953), 89-163.33.* (Figure 43)

Photograph of the furnace. After Nash-Williams, V.E. Archaeologia Cambrensis *102 (1953), 89-163.33.* (Figure 44a)

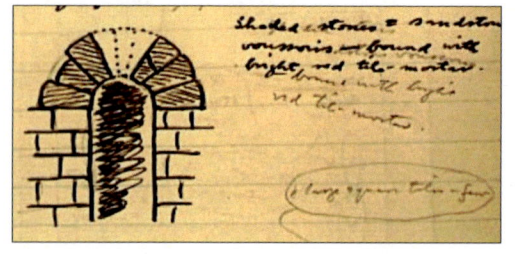

Nash-Williams sketch of the arched flue. (Figure 44b)

walled open yard area Rooms 32 and 33, and also the areas marked Rooms 34 and 35 on Figure 39. However, coal was also a possible fuel as the remains of coal stores have been uncovered at some Roman sites and coal was certainly used at this villa for iron smelting work in the workshops. The store yard areas were connected to a large rectangular basilican type building by a wall which had a sizeable opening, suggesting an access to the villa yard fronting the colonnade section. This might have been the grander entrance to the villa for use by visitors and guests and it may well have been gated. Arriving through this entrance, visitors would have been greeted by the sight of a substantial conjoined courtyard, the eastern section being utilised as a working area, whilst the western courtyard, flanking the colonnade was perhaps a garden area. A geophysical survey conduced in 2016, by Cardiff University and GeoArch, provided evidence of a possible wall running from the north-west corner of the Basilican building to the east side of Room 9 (a principal villa room). This would have separated the courtyards with a distinct division existing within the villa enclosure, of a higher status residential area to the western end and the lower status working yard fronting the workshops, basilican and barn buildings to the eastern end.

The Basilican Building

Basilican structures occur in association with Romano-British villas (particularly in the Wessex region) and functioned as workers and servant's quarters. The basilican at Llantwit villa was a substantial structure measuring approximately 97 feet long and 48 feet in width with exterior walls being 2 to 2.5 feet thick. Entrance was gained through doorways in the wall facing the courtyard, from Rooms 45 and 46, and an additional doorway in the west wall, at its south west angle. Internally, it was divided into a central nave, roughly 19 feet wide, separated from two flanking aisles 9 feet 6 inches wide by two substantial longitudinal walls 2 feet 6 inches wide. It was thought that their massive construction suggested that their function was to act as a base for two rows of columns supporting the nave roof. This idea was given plausibility by the discovery of a column-drum near the east end of the basilica that was probably part of such a column. The interior of the basilica building would have had a central colonnaded or clerestoried "nave" with flanking side aisles, presenting a medieval "church like" appearance. The standard basilican design was based on the first such structure, the Basilica Porcia, built in Rome circa 148 BCE, as a secular building to house meetings. Variations on the design, included an apse at one or both ends which were frequently used in judicial circumstances to accommodate magistrates on a raised platform. The early Christian church adopted basilicas for gatherings and modified the layout to include protrusions on each side to effect a cross like structure when viewed from above. The Llantwit Villa's basilican was roofed in a similar manner to the villa's other buildings with hexagonal or pentagonal roofing slabs. Unfortunately, due to a shortage of labour and time, Nash-Williams was unable to make a detailed clearance of the basilican building.

Many Roman villas had one such prominent aisled building which found use as a multifunctional area, not only to house large numbers of people and equipment, but also where indoor activities such as corn-drying could be conducted. Clearance of the eastern end of the central section (Room 44) of the Llantwit basilica revealed a roughly paved area with a complex of shallow channels built of course stone blocks, which may have acted as an installation for the parching of grain (Figure 45). In the southern part of the basilica (Room 43) clearance revealed a hollow sag in the floor surface near the north wall which contained a heavy deposit of charcoal, possibly originating from a hearth or brazier. The remains of oyster and mussel shells were discovered in the occupation layer of this area. This mirrors the discovery at Sparshot villa (Hampshire) where evidence suggests that a single cooking range surrounded by trampled food detritus and ashes, may have been part of a communal kitchen for workers residing in the basilican. The Llantwit Villa could have conformed to the general plan of the basilican format where part of one aisle would be partitioned for worker/family use whilst the other section would be used for drying grain, storage of produce, stabling and as seasonal shelter for farm animals.

The Eastern range

This consisted of two long rectangular buildings C and A separated by a passage providing an access to the eastern yard. Both buildings were substantial being approximately 78 feet long and 26 feet wide, with exterior walls of around 2 feet in thickness. Each was divided by an internal wall into two partitions of unequal size. Building C had an entrance onto the eastern courtyard through a doorway 4 feet 6 inches in width, whilst A had an entrance into the passageway between itself and building B. They were possibly acting as barns or stables for general farm purposes, such as storage or animal shelter. The roofs may have been constructed of stone slabs in keeping with the rest of the villa buildings, but a lack of evidence of such from the excavations could indicate the possibility of a wooden or thatched covering, which being far less durable would not have survived the ravages of time. The system of bank and ditch exterior to buildings C and A coincided with a gap midway along Building C which was possibly an entrance for a track. This would have allowed access to the villa's working areas through the passage above, for workers, and live stock.

The northernmost rectangular building comprised

workshops similar in style to that of Buildings C and A, measuring 72 feet long and 27 feet wide and connected to the villa Room 8 by three less substantial workrooms. This grouping of the workshops, used by the estate craftsmen, made them readily accessible from the entrance to the outer yard, and also well sited to discharge smoke from industrial activity away, from the main villa by the prevailing west, south-westerly winds. The presence of charcoal and iron clinkers provided evidence for their use in iron-working or smithying activities. A report on samples of the metallurgical remains by Mr A.D. Hopkins (Department of Metallurgy, University College, Cardiff), indicated that the probable method of smelting was to heap iron ore and coal in alternate layers, before covering with clay and then igniting the resulting mass. The ensuing rapid combustion of the coal aided by blasts of air to the centre of the mass, would reduce the iron oxide to iron which sank to the floor with its associated slag component. Pure iron could be refined from this mixture, and worked on anvils, as Storrie had proposed from his excavation of Room 1 in 1888 (Room 7 on the Nash-Williams plan). One area to the west of the northern range is of interest, as it's partial excavation suggested the possibility of further structure. This indeterminate segment is located in a relatively narrow area that is at the head of a shallow depression which slopes down to the present day water trough constructed over the spring Fynnon Caermead. Nash-Williams did not examine this section in detail, but Alexander Hogg in 1974 (see later) mentions that Storrie conducted some further excavations on this area, but did not publish his results. Hogg suggests that there are surface traces which indicate the remains of a wall enclosing another courtyard.

In common with the 1888 excavations, the numerous and varied items isolated during the course of the dig, reflected the everyday life of the occupants and the villa's working

Stone channels in the basilican building. (Figure 45)

environment. Pottery recovered from the villa was of two principal types, coarse and "Samian" ware. Some coarse pottery dated from the early iron age to medieval periods, but the overall majority was Roman, Caerleon "legionary" ware. This type of pottery is thought to have been produced by civilian potters near the Roman fortress of Caerleon. In 1996 excavations at the Celtic Manor resort Newport, revealed a kiln and several buildings (possible drying sheds) containing a range of broken Caerleon Ware at nearby Abernant Farm indicating pottery manufacture on a fairly large scale. The commonest types of course pottery recovered at the villa were flanged pie dishes, ollae (cooking pots), and amphorae (narrow necked two handled pot). Samian ware fragments from the villa were examined by Miss Grace Simpson M.A. of Hatfield College, Durham and found to be mainly of the Lezoux type. The Romans were well known for the introduction to Britain of red glossy pottery called *Terra Sigillata* ("Samian" ware) made in the south, east and central Gaul (modern Germany and France). Many of the main potteries were at Lezoux and La Graufesenque in France, and Rheinzabern in Germany. In addition to the Lezoux samples, found at the villa, some pottery pieces of quality exhibited the stamp (an eagle) of a potter that Simpson suggested may have been Cerialis of Rheinzaben.

Glass vessels also appear to have been in use at the villa. Dr. D.B. Harden of the Ashmolean Museum, Oxford, examined green glass vessel fragments recovered and determined that they belonged to cylindrical, or rectangular, bottles of the first to second centuries, whilst colourless fragments were thought to be from a cylindrical bottle of the third century. Numerous coins from the reigns of emperors such as Tetricus I (270-3 CE), Probus (276-81 CE), Carausius (286-93 CE), Constantine I (307-37 CE), Constantine II (317-50 CE), Constans (333-50 CE), Constantinus II (337-61 CE), were recovered. Miscellaneous finds included a second century T shaped brooch, bone pins, fragments of a bronze bangle, a knife handle made of deer antler, nails, Roman horse shoes and gaming counters. Animal remains included those of ox, pig, sheep, oyster, whelk, cockle, limpet, domestic fowl, and red deer which may be indicative not only of the husbandry of the villa but also the diet of the occupants. Domesticated animal remains included the horse and dog. A fragment of cuttle-bone discovered was found to be from the species *Sepia officinalis* the sac of which provided ink for Latin scribes for writing. Mr Lionel F. Cowley M.Sc who examined the human remains, discovered mainly in the northern range, found they were indicative of an age range from that of children to adults aged around fifty years. A small number of skeletal remains were reasonably intact with one belonging to a person aged thirty to forty years which exhibited severe arthritic crippling, and two others of females of around five feet in height.

Nash-Williams published his findings in the journal of the

Cambrian Archaeological Association, Nash-Williams, V.E. (1953) *Archaeologia Cambrensis*, Vol. CII, Part 2, pp. 89-163, detailing the excavations, artefacts found and a complete plan of the villa (Figure 33). He suggested a chronological sequence of the villa's construction, proposing five stages of development that described its lifespan. He conjectured that its construction began with the main residence living rooms, bath block, workshops, basilican and barns, which were founded around the middle of the second century CE. The zenith of prosperity occurred in the third century CE followed by an austere phase marking a change in the owners circumstances which saw a remodelling of the bath block, possibly to reduce running costs. Towards the end of the third century CE the main residence and bath block were abandoned, then stripped of its fittings and eventually dismantled. The industrial activity was transferred from the workshops to what remained of the baths which were then used for iron smelting. From this period onwards the residential occupation appears to have been confined to the basilican building. The occupants at that time, possibly having converted to Christianity, began burying their dead in the northern range which became a small cemetery. In the final stage, the basilican continued in use until the end of the fourth century CE and then was finally abandoned together with the cemetery. Thereafter, the site was considered to have been only occasionally occupied by medieval itinerants. His paper remained a definitive comment on Caermead until 1971, when another but, much smaller incursion of the site was made to reassess the villa's development.

Chapter 6

The 1971 Excavations

In 1971, the villa was to be included in the first volume of The Inventory of Ancient Monuments in Glamorgan, prepared for the Royal Commission on Ancient and Historical Monuments for Wales. A re-examination of the evidence from the previous excavations concluded that a number of assumptions pertaining to the villa's history needed reassessing. To address this, Alexander Hogg conducted a limited excavation to clarify some discrepancies pertaining to the sequence of the villa's construction. Hogg's excavation was limited in scope and confined to a re-excavation of Rooms 8 and 9, and a small excavation of the external junction of Rooms 16 and 17. Excavations began on 15th of November 1971 and were completed on the 22nd. By restricting his examination to those areas, Hogg attempted to minimise the effect of excavations on the site, considering that it was preferable to leave it buried and undisturbed. He published his findings in a paper with Dr D.J. Smith (Hogg, H.A.H and Smith, D.J (1974) 'The Llantwit Major Villa: A Reconsideration of the Evidence' *Britannia*, Vol. 5, pp. 225-250) in which he evaluated information from his excavations together with an re-examination of evidence accrued from previous work to re-appraise the villa's history. Accordingly he proposed a history for the villa which he considered to be consistent with the recorded data, but open to amendment in the light of new full scientific excavations. His hypothesis was the villa's history could be categorised in distinct periods of development.

Period I (three divisions to the beginning of the third century CE).

Ia. A pre-Roman settlement surrounded by a ditched enclosure.

The hypothesis for this local Iron Age connection is derived from a sherd of native Iron Age/Belgic pottery found on the site during the Nash-Williams excavations and also from excavations at Whitton Cross Roads, Barry. Here, the excavation of the Roman villa (dated to, circa second century CE) revealed that it was built over a rectangular Iron Age farmstead, which had been surrounded by a bank and ditch enclosure. The tentative suggestion is that both Caermead and Whitton villas may have developed from an original Iron Age settlement occupied by a local aristocratic class. When Romanisation occurred, these occupants maintained their social position, and embracing the Roman style, replaced their Iron Age roundhouses with the rectangular Roman villa.

Ib. Early Roman timber villa.

Ic. A simple rectangular (cottage block) block of some quality, constructed of masonry during the mid-second century CE.

This sequence of development is comparable to other villa sites, such as Lockleys, near Welwyn, Hertfordshire. Here, an original Iron Age round timber house was replaced by a Roman style wooden dwelling. This was eventually removed and a stone built strip house constructed which soon acquired two wings and a veranda to its front.

From the pottery evidence, Hogg concluded that Period I ended in the early third century CE. This was followed by a period of economic decline and of possible abandonment sometime during the middle of that century. He then proposed a second period of history for the villa.

Period II

Circa 270 CE the cottage block was rebuilt and extended with more structures being added during a phase of increasing prosperity. The culmination of this was the tessellated pavement in Rooms 8/9, which is the last event to which a date can be assigned. Period II can be divided into phases as below.

IIa. Enlargement of east end of the cottage block and nucleus of the west wing took place (circa 270 CE).

IIb. Structure linked and provided with the colonnade. Basilican building (B) and also Building A added. (circa 300 CE).

IIc. Maximum prosperity occurred circa 340-350 CE, indicated by insertion of the mosaic floor. The Basilican building may have fallen into disuse after the mid century.

IId. Continuing occupation but declining standards with bath suite being reconfigured, commencing with the reduction in size of the cold and hot baths.

Nash-Williams's report detailed that Room 27, the cold bath, experienced a reduction in size at some stage by the insertion of an inner wall 1 ft in thickness. In contrast to the original structure of large blocks and lime mortar, this was built of small stonework cemented with a sandy mortar and covered with a gritty red layer. A low wall 1 ft 3in in height, the top of which was mortared over to form a threshold, and seat, separated the *frigidarium* from the *piscina*. A step, 1 foot wide and situated 18 inches below the threshold acted as a second seat with a third, 9 inches wide and 10 inches high being set 1 foot 6 inches below the second. This configuration enabled the room to be filled with about 3 feet of water into which the bather could gradually descend by means of the steps. The hot bath room had also been reconfigured by the insertion of two walls of rough masonry, about 1 foot 8 inches wide positioned against the east and west walls. During this work the floor had also been replaced with one coloured deep pink-red. The reduction to both rooms were completed at roughly the same time possibly to conserve water, or simply to economise their running. The furnace (Room 31), underwent remodelling being reduced in size and capacity by insertion of a thick masonry layer against the west side of the fire-pit. In addition, the arched flue received a facing skin of tegulae reducing its size. These changes appeared to be concurrent with the cold and hot bath alterations, and infers a period of austerity for the villa. As the decline progressed, the stoking pit and fire hole were filled with stones and refuse, and the flue blocked with loose stones. These were placed deliberately, to make the furnace chamber redundant.

During the clearing of the *piscina*, the debris uncovered was of remarkable freshness which Nash-Williams considered to indicate that the bath apse had been deliberately demolished, rather than it experiencing a protracted decay. Further evidence for this conjecture came from the exterior of the bath's west wall. Here, the floor was found to be covered with a thick layer of debris, above which, the occupation layer showed signs of some form of activity continuing after the room was dismantled. Eventually, the wholesale dismantling of the bath suite rooms commenced. This was possibly carried out with a view to salvaging the valuable fittings such as hypocaust bricks, lead piping, glass windows etc. In the furnace room the presence of charcoal, pieces of coal and iron slag, together with a small clay bowl furnace 2 feet 6 inches in diameter, alluded to its eventual use as a workshop for metal working and smelting to replace those rooms of the northern wing. During this time the residential occupation also appears to have been transferred into the Basilican building of the southern range, which remained in use until sometime in the early fifth century. However, no date can be assigned to the final abandonment of the complex.

Hogg, proposed that there were two further incidents in the development of the site to which dates cannot be assigned, which he termed period III and IV.

Period III
After final abandonment, possibly a century later a band of around thirty persons (mainly men) were killed on site and their bodies left among the ruins.

Period IV
Site utilised as a Christian cemetery after buildings reduced to overgrown irregularities. This occurred around three hundred years after abandonment.

Hogg's limited excavation was the last incursion on the site, and his findings together with those of the previous excavations, conveyed an image of the villa's buildings and provided a timeline of its establishment, construction and eventual demise. The site had revealed a substantial structure of importance, not only in terms of the Romanisation of Wales, but also, of significance to the locality. Its size and grandeur hints that the idea of the villa being a solitary structure in the Vale of Glamorgan, is untenable and further local associated developments remain to be identified. Sadly, such an important archaeological site remains hidden from view, notwithstanding the Local History Society's attempt in 1981 to remedy this situation.

Chapter 7

The 1981 Attempt to Re-open Caermead

On the 27th July 1981, Mrs M.M.James, secretary of Llantwit Major Local History Society wrote to Dr Douglas Bassett, the Director of the National Museum of Wales inquiring about the possibility of re-opening the Roman Villa. Her letter was referred to George C. Boon, the Keeper of Archaeology and Numismatics, who informed Mrs James in his reply of the 3rd of August that the matter did not lie within the competence of the Museum. He advised her to approach, Dr M.W. Thompson, Principal Inspector of Ancient Monuments for Wales, at the Welsh Office in Cathays Park. Mr Boon's letter was somewhat negative, raising the question of finance, which he considered would be substantial, notwithstanding the continuing costs incurred in preservation of the exposed structure. Being undeterred by a pessimistic response, Mrs James accepted his advice and contacted Dr Thompson, who responded in a detailed letter of the 3rd of September, which reflected Mr Boon's position in offering little encouragement. Dr Thompson emphasised that the excavations conducted by Dr Nash-Williams were thorough, and it would be doubtful if any further intrusions of the site would add anything significant to the results already published in *Archaeologica Cambrensis* by Nash-Williams in 1953. He further stated that keeping the site open would be extremely costly and erecting protective buildings over them would entail an expenditure in the region of hundreds of thousands of pounds, notwithstanding the practical aspects involved, which he pointed out succinctly.

> *There is also the question of custody. Someone would have to look after the remains and allow the public in. The field in which the remains lie is privately owned and presumably would have to be purchased from the owner before any kind of work could be carried out. I do not think we are speaking of a practical proposal.*

Noting that government funds were available in certain circumstances he considered that they would not be applicable to the Llantwit site, since the high cost of displaying the ruins would hardly be justified. The pessimistic tone which pervades the letter, continues to the final paragraph.

> *I am afraid therefore I must be rather discouraging and say that so far as I can see the permanent display of the remains at Llantwit Major is not financially feasible. Unless you can persuade some American or Japanese millionaire to find very large sums of money I think the remains will have to stay as they are under the ground.*

This ironically, reflected the financial constraints that the Cardiff Naturalists' found themselves confronting nearly one hundred years earlier in pursuing their follow up explorations.

In November 1981, the Local History Society's guest speaker was Mr G. Dowdell, M.A, Director of the Glamorgan Gwent Archaeological Trust who spoke on the topic of "Romans and Natives in the Vale of Glamorgan. An illustrated introduction". Following this the Local History Society Committee, still undeterred by their recent disappointing approach to the Museum and Welsh Office, wrote to Mr Dowdell requesting information on Caermead. The request pertained to its protection by statute, acquisition by a Public Authority and the restoration of the site as an historical amenity. Mr Dowdell, having misplaced the letter only replied formally to the Secretary of the Society, Mrs M.James on 16th of June 1982.

> *Further to my lecture to your members some months ago I recently discovered a letter requesting information concerning the villa site at 'Caer Mead" (sic) which I had overlooked and not replied to. Please convey my apologies to members for my oversight in this matter.*

In his reply he addresses the three points raised in order, firstly stating that Caermead is fully protected from development and investigation by the recently introduced Ancient Monuments and Archaeological Areas Act. In response to the possible purchase by a Public Body, he endorses the view presented by Dr Thompson, that the economic climate was prohibitive, and as the site was currently being used for the grazing of livestock[1], it was in no danger whatsoever. From their third question, it appears that the Society despite their disappointment with the approach to the Welsh Office, were still keen for the site to be opened and restored as a local historical asset, in much the same manner as a number of other Roman villas in England had been. Mr Dowdell was unconvinced that restoration would be acceptable, based on what he described as a variety of sound archaeological reasons, such as the site having outstanding questions that needed detailed investigation, and its complexity, arising from different periods of development. He considered this a major factor in any restoration being able to accurately and realistically portray the villa. Once again, like Dr Thompson he concluded his letter with a pessimistic final paragraph.

> *I could forward an even greater number of objections, but feel that the above will probably suffice to ensure that the full realisation of many problems surrounding such a proposed course of action is appreciated by your members.*

Thus, despite the efforts of the Local History Society the villa site would remain, and still remains in much the same condition as Dr Nash-Williams left it after his 1948 excavation, with the only regular visitors being grazing livestock, quite oblivious to the fascinating history below their hooves.

The Decline of the Villa

From his 1888 excavations which revealed evidence of burnt timbers and bodies, Storrie made the assumption that the villa and its occupants had suffered a traumatic end, victims of barbarian Irish pirates. However, the dating of the human remains unearthed to the early medieval period casts doubt on that assumption. In addition, the charcoal remains of the burnt timbers of the villa roof could well be attributed to the fact that their presence in considerable volume would be a constant fire hazard, in buildings used for metal smelting activity. After the villa's abandonment, transient occupation by vagrants or travellers would only have increased the fire risk as they would be far less likely to be concerned about the buildings integrity than its owners. Nash-Williams findings that the bath-house was reconfigured to a smaller size before its eventual abandonment suggests that the Llantwit villa experienced a decline over an extended period, with less and less of the building being occupied as the economic environment worsened. As de-Romanisation increased so did the need for villa activities such as agricultural production, livestock output and tax rendering, leaving it increasingly redundant. Its last decaying function appears to have been as an early medieval cemetery, before that role also ceased and subsequently transferred, possibly to the nearby twelfth or thirteen century monastery and later the Church. All that remained for the villa was to be as a silent record of the incursion of a once great Mediterranean civilisation, that would eventually reveal its former grandeur to later generations through the intrusion of three physical excavations.

Principal Characters Involved with the Villa Excavations

John Storrie

John Storrie, the son of William and Agnes Storrie, was born in 1844 in Muiryett, in the parish of Cambusnethan, Lanarkshire, Scotland. He spent much of his youth in Glasgow where he can be found on the 1861 census living with his parents and three siblings at 171 Dobbies Loan, apprenticed to the printing trade as a Printer Compositor. It was during his youth that he developed an interest in local flora, winning a prize offered by a local merchant for the best collection of Scottish Alpine plants. His interest in natural history continued throughout his education in Glasgow where he eventually became acquainted with a Professor Page, an eminent geologist who's writings fuelled Storrie's enthusiasm for the sciences. He left Glasgow and undertook a fragmented journey south, with periods spent in Carlisle, Barrow and Manchester. Whilst resident in these towns he continued his studies of the local natural history, gaining considerable practical and theoretical experience. Arriving in Cardiff, around 1872 he continued his occupation in the printing trade, securing a position at the Western Mail's printing works, and pursuing his interest in natural studies by joining the local illuminati in the Cardiff Naturalists' Society. He subsequently left employment at the Western Mail in 1878 to become curator of the Cardiff Museum, but moved to the South of England for a short time during 1879. In his absence, the museum had two curators, Mr M.H.Cochrane and Mr

A.C.Cruttwell, F.G.S, who's brief tenure was followed by Storrie return to take up the post once more. He was certainly in post by the time of the 1881 census, taken on the 3rd of April, on which he is listed as a Museum Curator, residing at 182, Severn Road, Canton with his wife Augusta and two children, John and Agnes.

Under his tenure, the museum collections were classified and given an orderly manner as they expanded, whilst he also contributed to scientific advancement in the disciplines of botany and archaeology. Unfortunately, Storrie's personality was such that he was not adverse to engaging in disputes and grievances leading to a history of crossing swords with colleagues. One such instance saw him become embroiled in a grudge with the first librarian of the National Library of Wales, John Ballinger (1860-1933). Ballinger, was educated in Canton and at the Cardiff Science and Art Schools, becoming an apprentice at the Cardiff Free Library in 1875. His conflict with Storrie began during his time as assistant librarian, when Storrie found two youths fighting in the library magazine room, and marched them off to the local police station. On return to the library and unable to locate Henry Allpass the chief librarian, Storrie instructed Ballinger to deal with the matter. Ballinger, for whatever reason, did nothing and the two youths remained in custody for two days. The result was that Storrie received a public rebuke from the stipendiary magistrate, and considerable verbal admonishment from the Honorary Secretary of the Library, Mr Harries, who at the end of his rebuke saw fit to strike Storrie with his cane. Storrie's explosive personality erupted and he knocked the Honorary Secretary to the ground in response. The consequence of this was that Storrie apportioned full blame to Ballinger for the whole affair.

Storrie's smouldering resentment to Ballinger appears to have ignited a few years later over an incident involving the naturalist T.H.Thomas's discovery of some dinosaur footprints at Newton-Nottage, Porthcawl in 1878. The stone containing the footprints was entrusted to Storrie to make an impression and forward to London for identification. On completion, Storrie requested the Museum caretaker to clean up the mess in the cellar, but unfortunately no such thing happened. As a result Storrie became the recipient of a letter of admonishment, and he subsequently considered that Ballinger had engineered things to make him look entirely responsible. This incident was the catalyst for Storrie to resign as Curator and leave for the south of England in 1879. Ballinger left for Doncaster in 1881, and Storrie returned to the position of Curator at the Museum in the same year, believing that Ballinger was no longer a problem. However, in 1884 Ballinger returned to the museum as Chief Librarian, and as a consequence of the Free Library Committee being the controllers of the museum, he was now in a senior position to Storrie.

Storrie informed the committee that he would resign due to Ballinger's return. He was pacified by two honorary Free Library committee members, Peter Price and W.E.Winks, who indicated that Ballinger would have no authority over him if he agreed to withdraw his resignation. In 1885 Ballinger became secretary of the Cardiff Free Library Committee, and also secretary of the Cardiff Museum Committee and the Science and Arts School, which resulted in him acquiring power and influence. Once again, Storrie tendered his resignation and once more he was persuaded to stay in post, but as if by some fateful mischief, the vitriol continued to be fuelled by more incidents. During that year, coins which had been stolen from the museum were returned by post and found their way to Ballinger, who failed to inform Storrie. Ballinger subsequently denied, in front of two newspaper reporters, that they were in his possession, but eventually admitted the truth to Storrie. As with the Caermead vandalism incident, Storrie was not reticent in publicising his altercations and the whole of the Ballinger affair was cited by him in a letter to the Western Mail and published on 22nd April 1885. During his term as curator, he had experienced a troubled relationship with the Cardiff Free Library and also the Museum Committee. Mr John Ward, Storrie's successor at the museum, provided a hint in Storrie's obituary at the turbulent relationship Storrie had with the museum throughout his tenure there.

> *Why Mr Storrie resigned the curatorship in 1893 no one seems to exactly know. As his successor, I very naturally heard much of this resignation, but no two versions quite agreed. It appears to have been the outcome of many grievances, real or imaginary, extended over a considerable time.*
>
> *The museum—as most of the readers will be aware—was a delicate subject to touch upon with John Storrie.*
>
> (Ward, J. (1901-02) 'John Storrie', *Public Library Journal*, Vol. 3, pp. 81-84.)

Although he could rely on the support of many prominent members of Cardiff society, including distinguished academics, his influence with the upper echelons of Cardiff society resided almost entirely with the members of the Cardiff Naturalists', whom he relied upon for support. His resorting to publicise internal disputes through the press eventually alienated the Cardiff Free Library Committee, and his public sparring with Morien through the pages of the Western Mail did little to reduce his reputation for awkwardness and confrontation. His penchant for press appearances, causing irritation to his peers is evident from an entry in the Cardiff Naturalists' Society meeting minute book from 1894 during his excavations of the Roman villa at Ely. '*Resolved that in the case of the engagement of*

Mr Storrie to make the trial excavations, he be requested not to send communications to the press upon the subject.' (Cardiff Naturalists' Meeting Minutes 26th April 1894). Possibly, because of his humble background, although accepted, he never really fully absorbed into the circle of Cardiff Society, and may have always been regarded as an outsider. This is graphically portrayed in a cartoon, drawn by Herbert St Claire published in the Cardiff Figaro of 16th February 1892 (Figure 46). In it, Storrie is portrayed as a man of small stature standing behind, and eclipsed by, the imposing figure of Dr Charles Vachell, who is presenting a petition to a city dignitary calling for the separation of the Cardiff Free Library and Museum. The cartons implication is that Vachell is conducting the presentation of the partition, to his social equal, whilst Storrie, from a lower class is simply providing an artisan presence as merely a backdrop to the meeting with no possibility of any significant involvement. A passage in a letter by Thomas Jones director of Richard Jones and Company, Newport coal and shipping company and a member of the Cardiff Naturalists' Society, illustrates Storrie's situation with Cardiff's elite.

Storie is a splendid fellow but does not generally wear broadcloth and probably does not own a dress suit. The primary effect of the Cardiff Naturalists' is to afford members an opportunity for getting out their claw hammers...Our friend Dr Vachell even, who is one of the best of the lot, did not to my mind treat Storrie very well. He always appeared to me to adopt a patronising style to Storrie which was exceedingly offensive & also I think very much to take the kudos for what was really Storrie's work.
(Thomas Jones 1879)

Finally, in March 1893 Storrie resigned the curatorship of the museum, after the appointment of an assistant of whom he had a particular dislike. By 1895 he was suffering from mental health

Vachell and Storrie. From Cardiff Figaro 16th February 1892. (Figure 46)

problems whilst trying to make a frugal living as a dealer in philosophical and optical instruments. Robert Drane, the founder of the Cardiff Naturalists' Society, finding Storrie in poor health and financial difficulty, organised a committee of friends to assist. A sum of two hundred pounds, was raised which was presented to Storrie at a dinner in his honour at the Park Hotel, Cardiff on 16th May 1895 to help relieve his financial hardship.

During his career Storrie researched the botany of Cardiff and Glamorgan, publishing *"The Flora of Cardiff"* in 1886, engaged in geological work at Lavenock, unearthing a unknown species of *Mastodonsaurus* and undertook major archaeological investigations at Ely and Barry Island. He contributed articles to The Transactions of the Cardiff Naturalists' Society, and whilst working at the Silurian deposits at Rhumney he uncovered a unique algae which on submission to Kew Gardens was named *Nematophycus storriei* in his honour as the discoverer. He was the recipient of a prestigious award from the Geological Society of London and for his botanical work made an associate of the Linnean Society[1]. On the 1901 census, taken on the night of 31st March he is found living at 104 Frederick Street Cardiff with his wife Augusta and his children, John aged 25 a schoolteacher and Agnes aged 13 and is earning a living as a microscopist. Less than two months later, on May 2nd he died aged fifty seven of chronic bronchitis.

Charles Vachell

Charles Tanfield Vachell was a member of a prominent Cardiff family whose records can be traced back to around the year 1240 where they were resident in Berkshire. The Cardiff branch of the family was established by Charles Vachell (1784-1859) who moved there circa 1789, set up a druggist business, and married Margaret Redwood of Boverton House at Llanmaes church in 1811. His son John Redwood Vachell was the father of Dr Charles Tanfield Redwood Vachell (1848-1914). Charles Tanfield had developed an interest in botany as a boy and furthered this whilst attending Hereford Cathedral School, before reading medicine at London University. When settling into medical practice in Cardiff he continued his botanical interest by joining the Cardiff Naturalists' Society eventually becoming President on three separate occasions.

Mrs Murley

Ellen Wilkins, was the youngest daughter of Evan Wilkins of Great and Little Frampton and West Street Llantwit Major. She married Frederick Charles Vatchell in 1859, taking up residence in High Mead after William's death. Between them they had considerable wealth and could afford to employ some fourteen retainers. Frederick died in 1876 aged forty eight leaving Ellen and six children with considerable assets and she subsequently married a solicitor from Somerset, Hervey Murley.

Lord Bute (John Patrick Crichton-Stuart 3rd Marquess of Bute 1847-1900)

The Oxford University Alumni 1715-1886 lists him as matriculating on 13th of October 1865 aged eighteen years at Christchurch College. His education fostered his interest in architecture and scholarly pursuits, but in subsequent years his business acumen made him a considerable fortune for himself through his association with Cardiff docks and its export of Welsh Steam coal. Demand for this fuel became almost insatiable with the onset of the Industrial Revolution, with copious volumes being shipped through Cardiff, rewarding Bute's investment handsomely. He is best remembered in Wales for his association with William Burgess and their obsession with the medieval world, which catalysed their transformation of Cardiff Castle into a modern version of a castle with central heating and up to date plumbing. His archaeological interests resulted in a number of digs during the 1890's at the castle revealing Roman, medieval structures and a monastery, and he eventually left his business interests to others to attend to, whilst he pursued his archaeological and writing interests.

William Davies
Professor William Hopkin Davies was born in 1910 to Arthur and Catherine Davies (nee Hopkin), both of whom came from families with a long association with the town of Llantwit Major. William, was educated at Llantwit Major Elementary School, Barry Boys School and graduated from Cardiff University in Classics and Medieval History. After being awarded a Master of Arts degree he spent time in Rome and Harvard University before taking up a professorship at Aberystwyth in 1947, but still maintained a close association with Llantwit Major. It was intention to write a definitive work on the history of Llantwit Major during his retirement years, but unfortunately he suffered a disabling stroke and the project never came to fruition. He died in 1987.

V.E. Nash-Williams
Dr Nash-Williams was educated at Lewis School, Pengam and graduated from Cardiff University with a first class honours

Bachelor of Arts degree in 1922 and a Master of Arts in 1923. He was awarded a Doctor of Litteris in 1939 and spent his professional career at the National Museum of Wales and Cardiff University. With an interest in Roman and early Christian periods he was a keen excavator and conducted a number of digs at Sudbrook, Caerwent and Caerleon.

The Cardiff Naturalists' Society
The Cardiff Naturalists' Society had been formed in 1867 at the instigation of Robert Drane F.L.S[2] (1883-1914), with twenty four original members being recorded in the minutes. Early meetings being held in the Museum Room of the Cardiff Free Library, until the National Museum of Wales opened in 1927. The objectives of the society was the practical study of geology, the physical sciences and natural history, with an archaeology section being formed in 1894. It was the largest scientific society in Wales in 1905, the year it made representations to locate a National Museum in Cardiff, and it was a provider of testimonies in support of establishing a university college in Cardiff. One of its presidents (year of 1887), John Viriamu Jones became the first principle of the fledgling Cardiff University when it received a royal charter in 1884. Its annual transactions were published from 1868 to 1968 and the Society is still in existence today (2019) and has links with the National Museum of Wales.

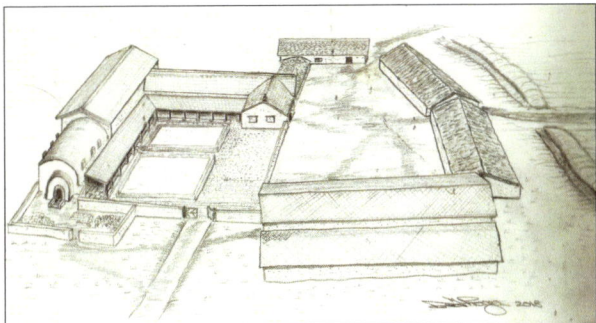

Artists impression of the villa circa 340 CE.

Notes

Introduction [1] The name "Caermead" is mentioned in various documents as Caer Mead, Caer Worgan Caer Wrgan etc. I have used the spelling Caermead as found on the modern ordinance survey map, throughout the text except where I have transcribed material from an original document. Here I have retained the spelling as written followed by (sic) to indicate such.

Chapter 1 [1] Sutton is approximately 3 miles north-north-west of Llantwit Major.

[2] The Downs is an area located to the west of Caermead and south of Sutton (Figure 3).

[3] Morien was the bardic name of Owen Morgan (1836-1921), a Welsh journalist at the Western Mail, Cardiff and a historian who wrote books on Welsh history and druidism. Much of his work was challenged by academics, and his 1903 publication *A History of Pontypridd and the Rhonda Valleys* was described by Robert Jenkins of Bangor University as "an odd jumble of Druidism and mythology".

[4] Theodosius I, Roman Emperor from 379 C.E to 395 C.E., was responsible for making Christianity the official religion of the empire, hence the reference to him in the newspaper article. Whilst Christian scholars credit him for this act, some historians consider him to have been a totalitarianism of the catholic faith, with his edict of Thessalonica, compelling all Christians to adhere to the catholic faith, or suffer the unpleasant consequences.

Chapter 2 [1] Lias is a term nineteenth century geologists used for hard limestone and also for a specific geological timespan, the early Jurassic epoch.

[2] Upchurch pottery is a type frequently associated with Romano-British pottery from a site of extensive potteries near the village of Upchurch, situated on the marshes at the mouth of the river Medway,Kent. The local clay from this area imparts a blue-black colour to the pottery.

[3] St Patrick

The young St Patrick was supposedly kidnapped by Irish pirates, during a raid on the coast of either Scotland or Wales. He spent a number of years in the north of Ireland as a shepherd before returning to his family in Britain. After religious training in France he was sent back to Ireland to engage in missionary work, converting the Irish to

Christianity, and allegedly preforming many miracles.

Chapter 3 [1] Illtud is also spelt Illtyd, and the church has been referred to by both variants in documents.

[2] The Duke of Teck, Francis Alexander was a member of the German nobility and took his title from Teck Castle located in the Dutchy of Swabia, Germany. He had little income in comparison to the majority of European princes and married into a richer family through his father's third cousin, Princess Mary Adelaide of Cambridge, a granddaughter of George III. Mary, known as "Fat Mary" due to extensive girth. When in her thirties, she was short of suitable suitors and thus the marriage appears to have been a convenient one for both of them, providing her with a titled husband and him with a wealthy bride. Their daughter, Victoria Mary (1867-1953) married George V.

[3] Storrie's original notes state that the name Caer Worgan was apportioned to the field on the authority of J. Stradling Carne. D.C.L of St Donats Castle when the 1877 survey was made by the Ordnance Surveyors. In a footnote to his paper on the excavations, published in the Cardiff Naturalists' Transactions, he states that the name Caer Worgan was to be removed from future O.S. editions due to the name being applied on insufficient grounds. The history of the the field had been traced back to the region of Queen Elizabeth by Mr Jas. Andrew Corbett, and in 1664 it bore the name of Lez Garnes, or stony field and then in 1799 Garne Meadow. The name Caer Mead appears to have originated from a corruption of Garn Mead or stoney meadow, whilst Caer Worgorn was allegedly an ancient name for Llantwit. Thus Stradling Carne imparted misinformation to the O.S. surveyors and as a consequence the field was named Caer Worgan in error.

[4] Augustus Henry Lane Fox Pitt-Rivers (1827-1900), was a noted archaeologist, responsible for innovations in archaeological methodology. His collection of over twenty thousand objects was the foundation of the Pitt Rivers Museum at Oxford University.

[5] Ernest Vachell died at sea on November 25th 1903, and thus unfortunately any plans he had envisaged did not come to fruition. Ernest's widow Joanna, married Mr E.T.Lloyd of Boverton court in 1910 to become Mrs E.T.Lloyd.

[6] The well, Ffynnon Caer-medd supplying the villa is certainly not located at the half way point between the villa and the property known as "The Downs", but a hundred yards or so west, from the villa bath complex.

Chapter 4
Chapter 5
[1] The names of the volunteers are those who's letters to Dr Nash-Williams survive in the archive in the Archaeology section of the National Museum of Wales, Cardiff.

[2] Enquiries with Utrecht University suggest that a likely candidate was Dr Jozua Johan Fraenkel who matriculated in 1932, graduated on 7/7/1937 with a bachelors degree and a Ph.D on 10/5/1940 (the day of the German invasion). In Holland Joop is a short form of the name Johan.

[3] There is no direct evidence of which excavation season Dr Fraenkel took part in.

[4] Marie Trevelyan was the pen name of Emma Thomas (1853-1922) the daughter of Iltyd and Mary Thomas of Llantwit Major. She used her married name, Madame Paslieu (pronounced "Paloo") for some of her later work. Between 1893 and 1896 she produced a trilogy of books, one of which "Glimpses of Welsh Life and Character" was dedicated (with permission) to H.R.H the Duchess of York, who as Princess Mary of Teck had signed the visitors book during her visit to the 1888 excavations at Caermead. Her smallest publication was the one mentioned in Mr George's letter, "*Llantwit Major. Its History and Antiquities*", which relied heavily on the now challenged Iolo Morganwg's researches, and spanned the Pre-Roman period through to the early nineteenth century. See Williams, N. (2008) 'Marie Trevelyan: An Authoress With Three Names' *Llantwit Major, Aspects of its History*, Vol. 8, pp. 54-69. Llantwit Major Local History Society.

[5] The use of labourers to remove top-soil was quite acceptable during that time, but not regarded as good practice now.

[6] A large percentage of the structure, including both courtyards and rooms still remain un-excavated.

Chapter 6
Chapter 7
[1] Livestock, grazing on the site of the villa affords protection by maintaining an environment free of shrubs and trees, the roots of which can cause damage to ancient buried structures.

Principle Characters involved with the villa Excavations
[1] The Linnean Society is the world's oldest active biological society, founded in London in 1788 and named after the Swedish botanist Carl Linnaeus (1707-1788), Chair of Medicine at Uppsala University, Sweden, who devised the definitive botanical naming system.

[2] Fellow of the Linnean Society.

Further Reading

Andrews, H. (1930's) Diaries. Llantwit Major local History Archive.

Hogg, H. A. H. and Smith, D. J. (1974) 'The Llantwit Major Villa: A Reconsideration of the Evidence' *Britannia*, Vol. 5, pp.225-250.

Manning, W. (2001) *A Pocket Guide Roman Wales*, Cardiff, University of Wales Press and The Western Mail.

Nash-Williams, V. E. (1953) 'The Roman Villa at Llantwit Major in Glamorgan', *Archaeologia Cambrensis*, Vol. CII, Part 2, pp. 89-163.

Storrie, J. (1888) Original Notebook, Llantwit Major Local History Archive.

Storrie, J. (1888) 'Report on the Excavations Near Llantwit Major', *Cardiff Naturalists' Society Report and Transactions*, Vol. XX, Part II, p. 49.

Williams, N. (2008) 'Marie Trevelyan: An Authoress With Three Names', *Llantwit Major Aspects of its History*, Vol. 8, pp. 54-69.

Young, C. (2004) 'Professor W. H. Davies' *Llantwit Major Aspects of its History*, Vol. 4, pp. 95-101.

Young, C. (2007) 'The Wilkins Family of Llantwit Major, and the Land They Acquired', *Llantwit Major Aspects of its History*, Vol. 7, pp. 40-49.

Young, C. (2007) 'The Vachell Family of Cardiff and the Dispersal of the Wilkins Land', *Llantwit Major Aspects of its History*, Vol. 7, pp. 50-61.

Dr Nash-Williams 1953 paper is now available online on the Welsh Journals Online website:

https://journals.library.wales/view/4718179/4741564/116#?xywh=-1753%2C-7%2C6439%2C3941

Acknowledgement for Figures

Figures 1, 2, 3, 11 and 27 and Roman villa sketch D.T. Rogers.

I am extremely grateful to the following organizations for their assistance and permissions for the use of images in the following figures.

Figures 5, 8, 9, 15, 16, 18 and 19. Reproduced by kind permission of Cardiff Naturalists' Society.

Figures 23, 26, 31, 32, 33, 34, 35, 36, 38, 39, 40, 41, 42, 43, 44a and 45. Reproduced by kind permission of the Cambrian Archaeological Association.

Figures 6, 7, 10, 12, 13, 14, 17, 20, 22, 24, 28 and 37. Reproduced by kind permission of Llantwit Major History Society Archive.

Figures 21, 25, 29, 30 and 44b. Reproduced by kind permission of the National Museum of Wales, Cardiff.